I0113816

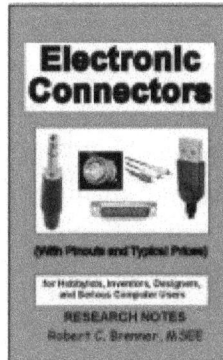

ELECTRONIC CONNECTORS
(With Pinouts and Typical Prices)

For hobbyists, experimenters, designers and serious computer users
Robert C. Brenner, MSEE

ISBN 978-1-930199-79-8

NOTICE: Fair Use Copyright Disclaimer

"Under Section 107 of the Copyright Act 1976, allowance is made for "fair use" for purposes such as criticism, comment, news reporting, teaching, scholarship, and research. Fair use is permitted by copyright statute that might otherwise be infringing. Non-profit, educational, research, or personal use tips the balance in favor of fair use."

Any use of copyrighted material is done for research, comment, or educational purposes. The publisher does not endorse any product, place, or person inferred by creators of copyrighted material presented herein for criticism, comment, research, or educational purposes under the Fair Use allowance quoted above.

CAUTION

Electricity can be dangerous if handled carelessly. But respect it, deal with it carefully, and electricity will give you a lifetime of service. So follow all cautions, warnings, and other notes published in the literature provided by the manufacturers and government standards organizations.

INTRODUCTION

I was seeking an adapter to connect a ZIP250 drive to my computer so I could access over a dozen disks that contained documents and files I had previously saved. I was unable to locate the ZIP data adapter. So I began researching. I found little information on ZIP products. I checked libraries and online sources. There was nothing listed in any library and the largest online retailer had only four books on connectors—all from years ago and all used. Worse yet, the prices were between $74 and $380 for a *single copy*. I immediately recognized a need for a affordable reference that we could use today.

A connector is an electromechanical device that joins two electrical parts.

The pins on the plugs and in the sockets are assigned specific signals or voltages, so pinout assignment diagrams were created to show what each pin is for.

When the digital era began, we needed connectors that could handle higher data rates and complex signals. Advances in connector technology moved at fast speed all through the late 50s and 60s as designers developed connectors that enabled us to hook peripheral devices to a myriad of computers. Thus the D-sub, HDMI, SCSI and USB were introduced. .About one-third of electronic connectors sold in the U.S today are for printed circuit boards. And a strong demand for miniaturization continues to drive technological advances in the market. The shrinking size of new components requires heavy investments in specialized machines able to make new connectors.

Computer hardware now can operate at speeds of 500 to 800 MHz with pulse rise times of 50 to 120 picoseconds, and transmission speeds greater than 580 megabits per second (Mbps). Yet, the shorter distances (less than 30 meters – about 100 feet) make fiber optics not significantly applicable, so connector technology continues to focus on developing technologies that are compatible with copper fiber channel cabling.

The drive for miniaturization was also fueled by the laptop computer industry, which required high density interconnections for miniaturized memory cards, 1.8-inch disk drives, and connectors for linking the laptops to networks and desk-based PCs. Two-millimeter to 0/8mm connectors were developed for use in the smallest of computers and pagers. However, newer designs were required as applications for electronic components demanded smaller, conveniently sized and weighted apparatus. Traditional manufacturing processes were using traditional technologies that utilized mated receptacle and plug pairs. Newer designs featured connectors that did not require a receptacle.

In the 50s and 60s, most connectors were roughly similar to the D-Sub design used for RS-232. A stiff, straight pin engaged a springy socket that contacted and bore against it on all sides. There were minor variations in shape and placement, but they were all variations on the same theme.

Users found that the female connector would be the one to break, so they used females only on cables, because they were easier to repair

As the communication revolution continues, our electronic future looks bright. Electronic connectors have become the game-changers.

COMPUTER INTERFACE SOCKETS

Each computer—desktop, tower or laptop—has interface sockets built into its chassis. These sockets provide ways to connect to peripheral devices such as printers, scanners, or displays. Here are interface sockets I found on computers being sold today.

3.5mm audio
3.5mm HP/MIC TRRS
5.5mm DC Port
DB9
DB15
Display Port
Ethernet
HDMI
Headphone audio
Micro SD slot
Microphone audio
PS/2
RJ45
Serial printer port
USB 2.0
USB 3.0 Type A Gen 1
USB 3.0 Type A Gen 2
USB 3.1 Gen 1
USB 3.1 Gen 2
USB 3.2 Gen 1
USB 3.2 Type C
VGA

COMMON CONNECTORS

After considerable thought (and hours and hours of research), I decided the best way to cover this subject is to list all the components I could find, and then show each with graphics and pin assignments. Where I could, I showed a typical price for these. Concurrently, I developed a Glossary with extensive research notes. (email rcbwrites@gmail.com for purchase details).

Here are pinouts for connectors with dedicated pins.

DB9

Purpose - a serial connector for keyboards, mice, joysticks and data cables.

Graphic -

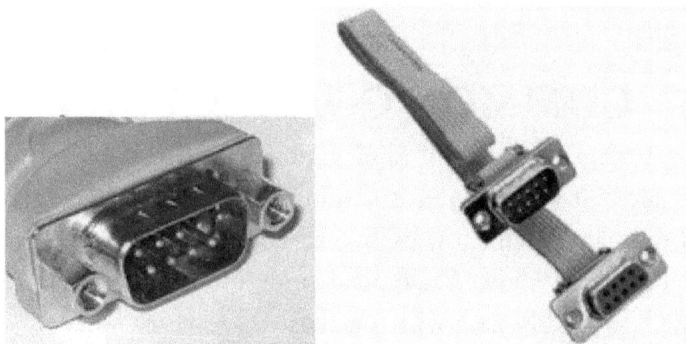

Fig. 1 – DB9 connector

Pinout -

DB-9F

DB9 Pin Assignments
1 - Relay 3 Common
2 - Relay 3 (normally closed)
3 - Relay 3 (normally open)
4 - Relay 4 Common
5 - Relay 4 (normally closed)
6 - Relay 4 (normally open)
7 - Input A2
8- Input B2
9 - 12V
(Shield 0V)

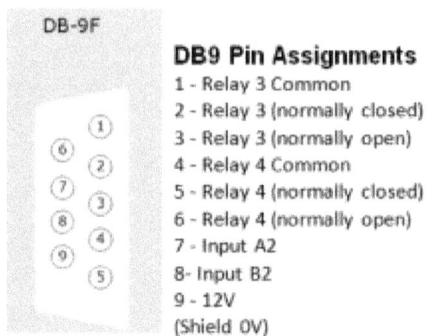

Fig. 2– DB9 connector pinouts

Adaptor	MDA	CGA	EGA
		9-pin connector pinouts	
Pin 1	Ground	Ground	Ground
Pin 2	Ground	Ground	+ Secondary red (intensity)
Pin 3		+ Red	+ Red
Pin 4		+ Green	+ Green
Pin 5		+ Blue	+ Blue
Pin 6	+ Intensity	+ Intensity	+ Secondary green (intensity)
Pin 7	+ Video	Reserved	+ Secondary blue (intensity)
Pin 8	+ Horizontal sync. (18.43 kHz)	+ Horizontal sync. (15.7 kHz)	+ Horizontal sync. (15.7 / 21.85 kHz)
Pin 9	− Vertical sync. (50 Hz)	+ Vertical sync. (60 Hz)	± Vertical sync. (60 Hz)

Fig.3– 9-pin connector pinouts

Typical Price – $5.95 - $10.99

DB15

Purpose – a connector for automatic control and industrial control equipment, cash registers, tax control machines and high-quality signal transmission between desktop computers, notebooks, all-in-ones, HD DVDs, digital HD set-top boxes, X-BOX360/PS3, game consoles, digital cameras, camcorders, LCD HD projectors, LCD monitors, VGA and high-definition digital TVs.

Graphic -

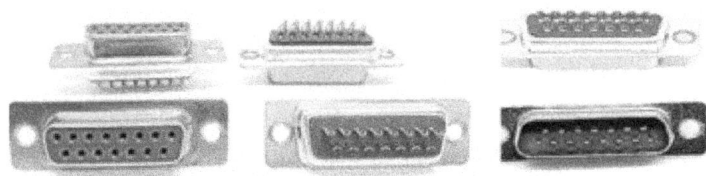

Fig. 4 – DB15 connector

Pinout –

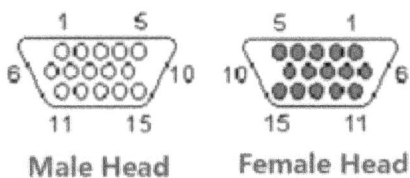

Male Head   Female Head

VGA male connector

DB15 Pin Assignments

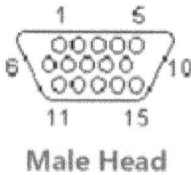

Pin	Name	Description
1 - VGA Red	Red Video
2 - VGA Green	Green Video
3 - VGA Blue	Blue Video
4- GND	Signal Ground
5 - Red_RTN	Red Ground
6 - Green_RTN	Green Ground
7 - Blue_RTN	Blue Ground
8 - VDC	5 Vdc supply (fused)
9 - GND	Signal Ground
10 - SDA	DDC.12C data
11 - HSYNC	Horizontal sync
12 - VSYSC	Vertical sync
13 - SLC	DDC/12C Clock

Male Head

Fig 5 – DB15 connector pinouts

Typical Price – $9.59 - $13.99

DB25

Purpose - a parallel connector for older printers.

Graphic -

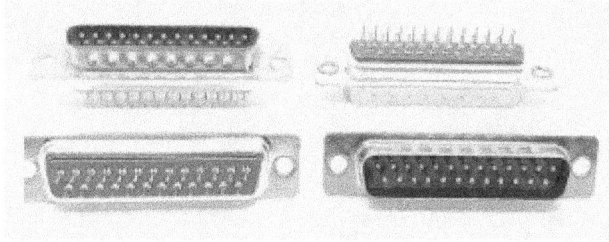

Fig.6 – DB25 connector

Pinout - 8 data out pins, 4 output control pins, 5 input control pins, and 8 ground pins; operating voltage 5.0Vdc.

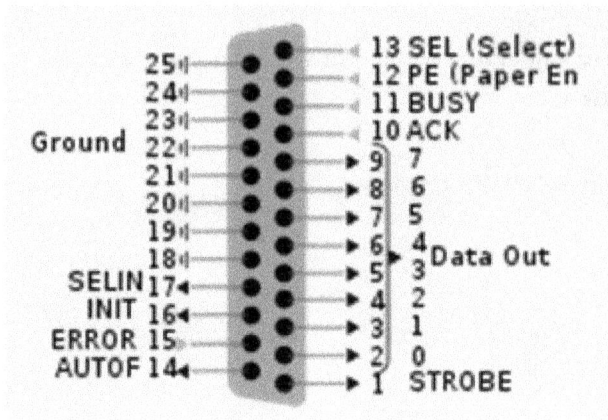

DB25 Pin Assignments

1 - Strobe out
2 - 0 out   Data Out
3 - 1 out   Data Out
4 - 2 out   Data Out
6 - 3 out   Data Out
6 - 4 out   Data Out
7 - 5 out   Data Out
8 - 6 out   Data Out
9 - 7 out   Data Out
10 - ACK in
11 - BUSY in
12 - PE in   Paper En
13 - SEL in   Select
14 - AUTOF out
15 - ERROR in
16 - INIT out
17 - SELIN in
18 – not connected
19 – not connected
20 – not connected
21 – not connected
22 – GND in   Signal Ground
23 – not connected
24 – not connected
25 – not connected

Fig. 7 – DB25 connector pinouts
Typical Price – $11.97 - $14.99

————————————————————

DB37

Purpose – a serial connector for computers, barcode machines, control machines, digital cameras; PDAs, modems, set-top boxes, industrial instrumentation and other communication equipment.

Graphic -

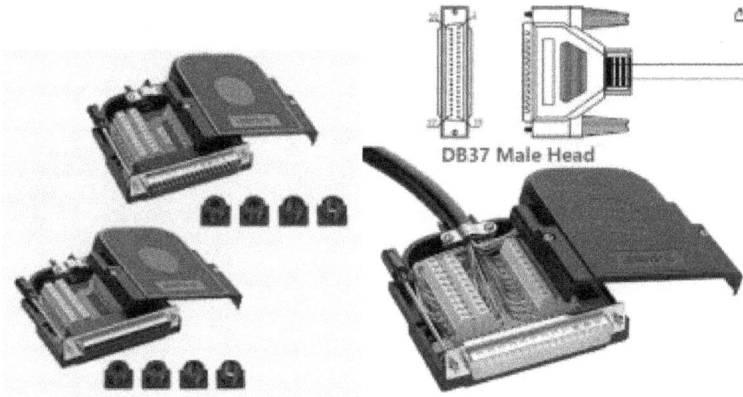

Fig. 8 – DB37 connector

Pinout –

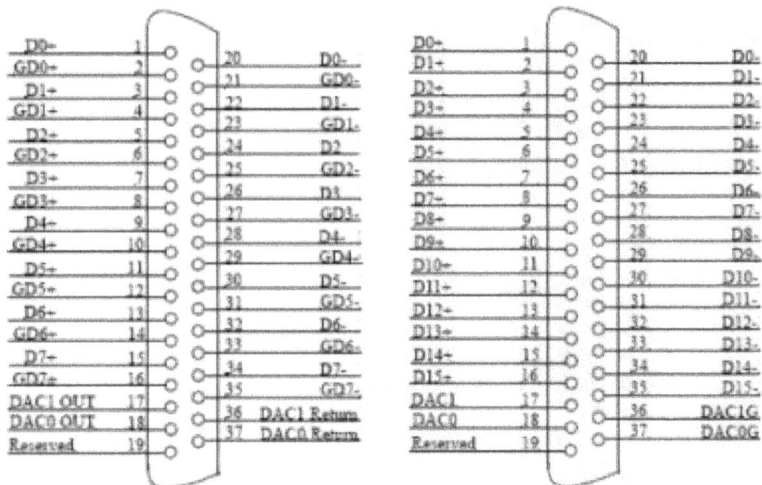

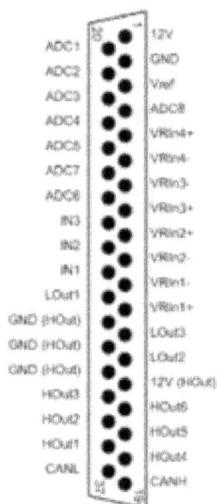

DB37 Pin Assignments

1 - 12V	1 - D0+
2 - GND	2 - D1+
3 - Vref	3 - D2+
4 - ADC8	4 - D3+
5 - VRin4+	5 - D4+
6 - VRin4-	6 - D5+
7 - VR3-	7 - D6+
8 - VR3+	8 - D7+
9 - VR2+	9 - D8+
10 - VR2-	10 - D9+
11 - VR1-	11 - D10+
12 - VR1+	12 - D11+
13 - LOut3	13 - D12+
14 - LOut2	14 - D13+
15 - 12V (HOut)	15 - D14+
16 - HOut6	16 - D15+
17 - HOut5	17 - DAC1
18 - HOut4	18 - DAC2
19 - CANH	19 - (Reserved)
20 - ADC1	20 - D0-
21 - ADC2	21 - D1-
22 - ADC3	22 - D2-
23 - ADC4	23 - D3-
24 - ADC5	24 - D4-
25 - ADC6	25 - D5-
26 - ADC7	26 - D6-
27 - ADC8	27 - D7-
28 - IN2	28 - D8-
29 - IN1	29 - D9-
30 - LOut1	30 - D10-
31 - GND (HOut)	31 - D11-
32 - GND (HOut)	32 - D12-
33 - GND (HOut)	33 - D13-
34 - HOut3	34 - D14-
35 - HOut2	35 - D15-
36 - HOut1	36 - DAC1G
37 - CANL	37 - DAC0G

Fig. 9 – DB37 connector pinouts

Typical Price – $19 - $37

————————————————————————

DIN

Purpose – **a** connector for various home computers and video game consoles, for interfacing SYNC or MDI, for peripherals or power connectors, model aircraft radio controllers and for older 16mm movie projectors.

Graphic -

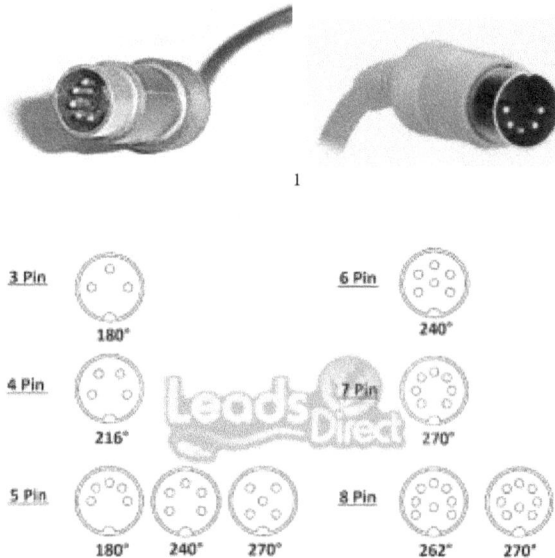

Fig. 10 – DIN connector

Pinout –

---

1. https://en.wikipedia.org/wiki/File:5pin180dinplug.jpg

Application		Connector	Pin function				
			1	4	2	5	3
Amplifier	Monophonic	5/180°	Audio out			Audio in	
	Stereophonic		Left out	Right out	Screen/return	Right in	Left in
Tape recorder	Monophonic		Audio in			Audio out	
	Stereophonic		Left in	Right in		Right out	Left out
Common colors on DIN-4*RCA adapters			white	red		yellow	black
Common colors on DIN-2*RCA adapters			(sometimes joined with pin 5)			red	white

DIN-5/180 Amplifier (Stereophonic)

1 - Left out
2 - Screen/Return
3 - Left in
4 - Right out
5 - Right in

Fig. 11 – DIN connector pinouts

Typical Price – $1.74 - $2.00

———————————————————————

FireWire (IEEE 1394)

Purpose – an interface standard for serial bus high-speed (400 MBps) communications and real-time data transfer for digital cameras. FireWire can handle 400-3200 MBps with 30V max voltage and 1.5A max current.

Graphic -

Fig. 12 – Symbol for IEEE 1394 FireWire interface

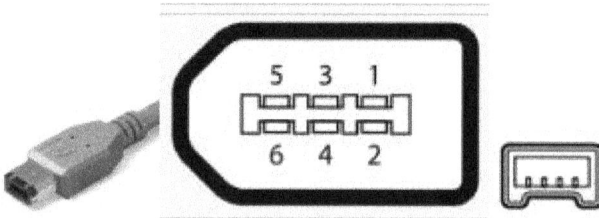

USB Type A

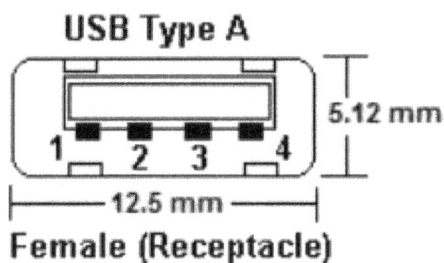

5.12 mm

12.5 mm

Female (Receptacle)

Firewire 800 (IEEE 1394b)

9 8 7 6 5

1 2 3 4

9 pin Female (Receptacle)
Bilingual or Beta

Fig. 13 – FireWire connector

Pinout – (Also see manufacturer's specs and Glossary in this book.)

4 pin, 6 pin or 9 pin IEEE1394 (FireWire) plug connector

Defined by IEEE 1394-1995 standard as a serial data transfer protocol and interconnection system. Also known as iLink (Sony) or Lynx. Often implemented in consumer electronics devices, digital video cameras, VCRs, some other multimedia hardware and computers.

4-pin connector	6-pin connector	9-pin connector	Name	Description	color of wire in cable
	1	8	Power	Unregulated DC; 30 V no load	white
	2	6	Ground	Ground return for power and inner cable shield	black
1	3	1	TPB-	Twisted-pair B, differential signals	red
2	4	2	TPB+	Twisted-pair B, differential signals	green
3	5	3	TPA-	Twisted-pair A, differential signals	orange
4	6	4	TPA+	Twisted-pair A, differential signals	blue
		5	A shield		
		7		-	
		9	B shield		
Shell			Outer	cable shield	

6-pin	4-pin	Function
1		Power (~30V)
2		Ground
3	1	Twisted pair B- (send data)
4	2	Twisted pair B+ (send)
5	3	Twisted pair A- (receive data)
6	4	Twisted pair A+ (receive)

Signal Name	PIN OUT IEEE 1394 6P/M	Cable
+5 Ext	1	White
Gnd	2	Black
Analog 1	3	Orange
Analog 1 Gnd	4	Blue
Analog 2	5	Red
Analag 2 Gnd	6	Green

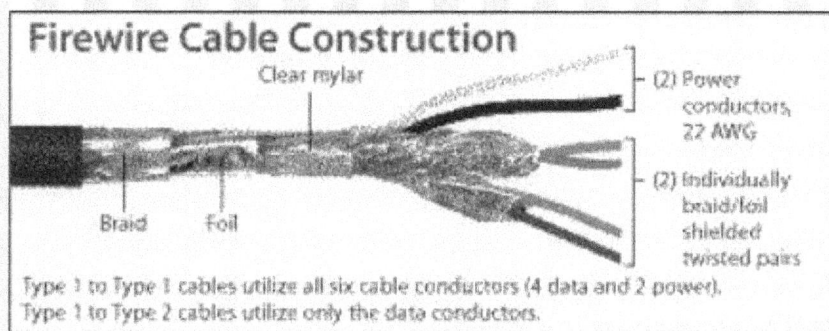

Firewire Cable Construction

Clear mylar

(2) Power conductors, 22 AWG

(2) Individually braid/foil shielded twisted pairs

Braid   Foil

Type 1 to Type 1 cables utilize all six cable conductors (4 data and 2 power).
Type 1 to Type 2 cables utilize only the data conductors.

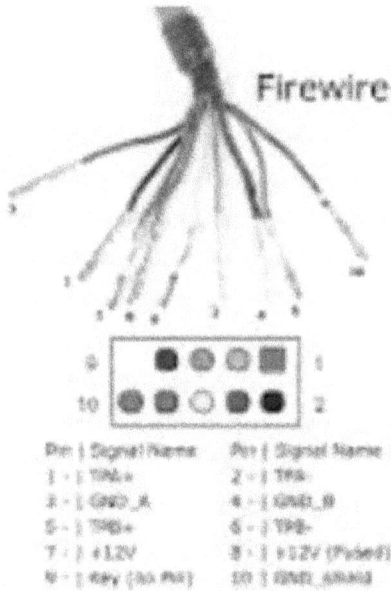

Fig. 14 – FireWire connector pinouts
Typical Price – $6.26 - $13.99

——————————————————————

HDMI (HDMI (High Definition Multimedia Interface)

Purpose – a compact standard for transmitting uncompressed simultaneous audio and video digital data. HDMI can also be used purely for either audio or video signals. This is useful because, with the addition of the right adaptor, it allows HDMI cables and connectors to link hardware devices with a number of different port types.

Graphic -

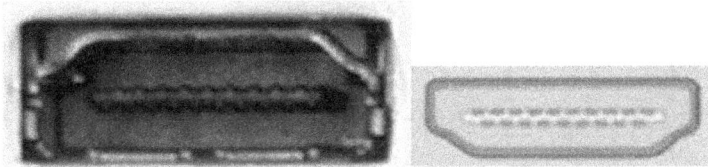

HDMI Type A socket

Fig. 15 – HDMI connectors

Pinout –

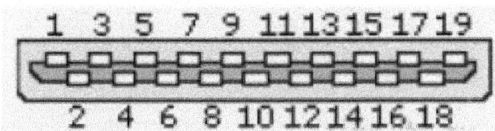

ROBERT C. BRENNER

Pin	Signal	Description
3	TMDS Data2+	
4	TMDS Data2 Shield	
5	TMDS Data2-	
6	TMDS Data1+	
7	TMDS Data1 Shield	
8	TMDS Data1-	
9	TMDS Data0+	
10	TMDS Data0 Shield	
11	TMDS Data0-	
12	TMDS Clock+	
13	TMDS Clock Shield	
14	TMDS Clock-	
15	CEC	control
2	Utility/HEAC+	N.C. on device
17	SCL	DDC clock
18	SDA	DDC data
16	DDC/CEC/HEAC Ground	
19	+5 V Power	power EDID/DDC
1	Hot Plug Detect/HEAC-	

HDMI

DATA
+5V
+6VI
+7VII
ANTIDATA
WATER
VACUUM
AMAZON
COPYRIGHT PIN
DECORATIVE

+3.3V DC
-3.3V DC
Tx
WX
Rx ONLY
UNKNOWN
+240V DC
5V AC
GND
GROUND

MICRO USB

white   black   GND   blue   brown

red   GND   white   green   GND

[1] [3] [5] [7] [9] [11] [13] [15] [17] [19]

[2] [4] [6] [8] [10] [12] [14] [16] [18]

GND   white   green   white   red

blue   GND   white   brown

HDMI

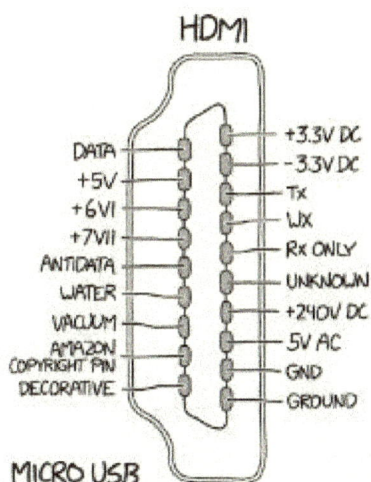

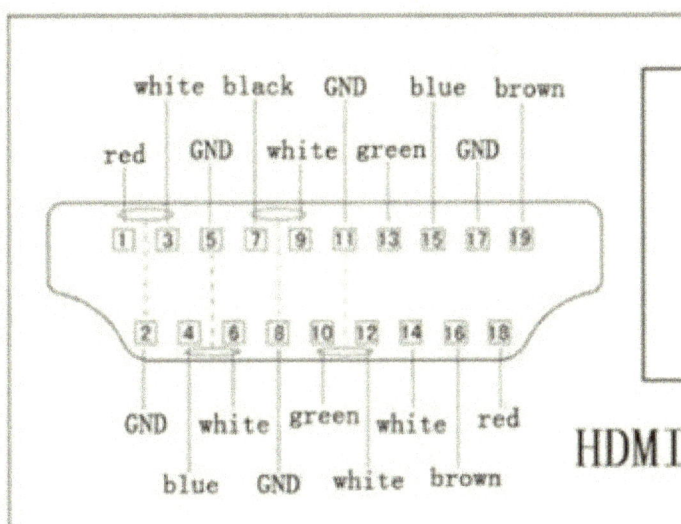

Fig. 16 – HDMI connector pinouts
Typical Price – $1.88 - $10.99

J1708

Purpose - a serial connector for communications between an electronic control unit (ECU) and other components on a heavy duty vehicle and also between a computer and the vehicle.

Graphic -

J1708

Fig. 17 – J1708 connector

Pinout -

Six-Pin Diagnostic

A - J1708 Data Link +
B - J1708 Data Link -
C - Power
E - Ground

Fig. 18 – J1708 connector pin assignments

Typical Price – $18.99 - $35.00

J1939

Purpose – a connector that enables an Electronic Control Unit (ECU) to transmit data over a Controller Area Network (CAN) in a heavy-duty vehicle – bus; truck, tractor, or industrial machine.

Graphic -

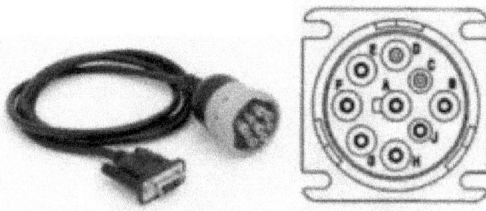

Fig. 19 – J1939 connector

Pinout –

Pin	Type 2 (Green)
A	Ground
B	Battery
C	J1939 + 500kb
D	J1939 - 500kb
E	J1939 Shield
F	J1708+ / J1939 + 250kb
G	J1708- / J1939 - 250kb
H	OEM Specific
J	OEM Specific

Fig. 20 – J1939 connector pin assignments
Typical Price – $14.99 - $18.99

M8

Purpose – a cylindrical, multi-pin electrical connector that transmits both data and power. Common applications include actuators, PLCs, I/O boxes, sensors, and switches in food and beverage processing, machine building, rubber and plastics, textile and printing presses and in HVAC system valves.

Graphic -

Fig. 21 – M8 connector

Pinout -

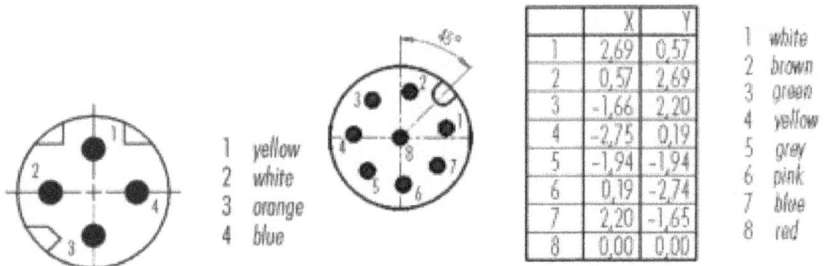

1	yellow
2	white
3	orange
4	blue

	X	Y
1	2,69	0,57
2	0,57	2,69
3	-1,66	2,20
4	-2,75	0,19
5	-1,94	-1,94
6	0,19	-2,74
7	2,20	-1,65
8	0,00	0,00

1	white
2	brown
3	green
4	yellow
5	grey
6	pink
7	blue
8	red

Fig. 22 – M8 connector pin assignments

Typical Price – $7.99 - $14.79

————————————————————

M12

Purpose - A circular connector with a 12-mm locking thread used primarily in factory automation applications for actuators, sensors, industrial Ethernet and Fieldbus.

Graphic –

Fig. 23 – M12 connector

Pinout - Choosing the right M12 connection depends on your specific application. M12 connections come in a variety of pin positions, anywhere from 2, 3, 4, 5, 6, 8, 12 and 17 pins. The number of pins varies depending on the signal type and number of signals, connection coupling and code.

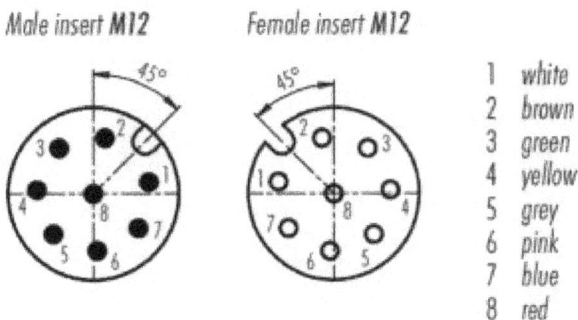

Male insert **M12**   Female insert **M12**

1	white
2	brown
3	green
4	yellow
5	grey
6	pink
7	blue
8	red

Fig. 24 – M12 connector pin assignments

Typical Price – $13.99 - $18.99

MC3

Purpose – interlocking plugs with 4mm diameter contacts for connecting solar panels.

Graphic –

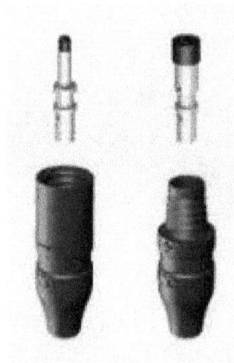

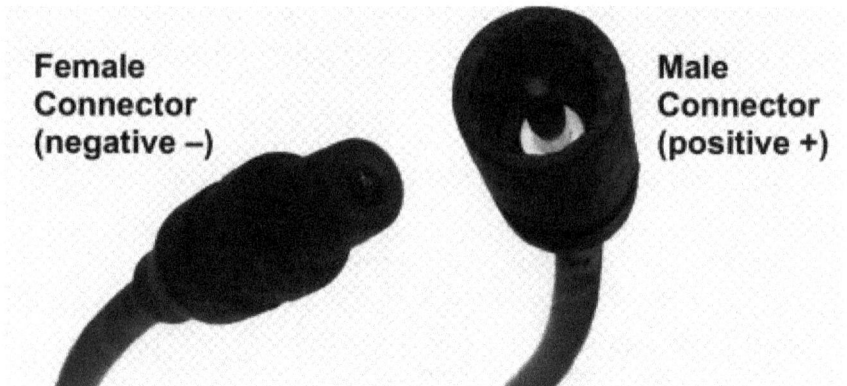

Fig. 25 – MC3 connector

Pinout – The female connector is the negative side of the cable. The male connector is the positive side.

Typical Price – $7.99 (6 pairs) - $12.49 (5 pairs)

MC4

Purpose - Single-contact electrical connector commonly used for interfacing solar panels..

Graphic –

Fig. 26 – MC4 connector

Pinout – The positive (+) wire has a female MC4 connector and the negative (-) wire has a male MC4 connector. For smaller panels (such as stand-alone walkway lights), often the wires are red and black. The red ring marks the positive connection. The black wire is for the negative connection.

Typical Price – $7.99 (6 pairs) - $14.99 (2 pairs)

Micro-D

Purpose - Smaller connectors derived from the D-sub design with primary applications in military and space-grade technology.

Graphic -

Comparison of microminiature (Micro) D connector and male DB-9

Fig. 27 – Micro-D connector

Pinout – (See manufacturer's specs.)

Typical Price – $20.99 - $175.23

Micro-HDMI (Micro High Definition Multimedia Interface)

Purpose – to transfer uncompressed digital signals from any suitable audio-video (A/V) source to the receiver or display device it's plugged in to. Links desktop computers to monitors, TVs to set-top boxes and games consoles to projectors

Type D HDMI connectors are the micro versions. These are smaller than both standard and mini HDMI connectors, but retain the same 19-pin configuration (albeit in a slightly different layout due to the micro format size constraints).

Type D micro HDMI connectors measure just 5.83mm × 2.20mm, which makes them similar in overall size to a micro-USB connector, and less than half the size of a standard HDMI Type A plug or socket. Type D was developed specifically for audio-video connectivity in very small, highly portable devices such as mobile phones.

Graphic –

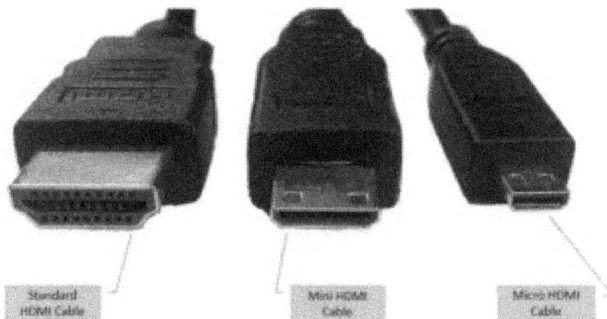

Standard HDMI Cable   Mini HDMI Cable   Micro HDMI Cable

Micro HDMI
Fig. 28 – Micro HDMI connector

Pinout -

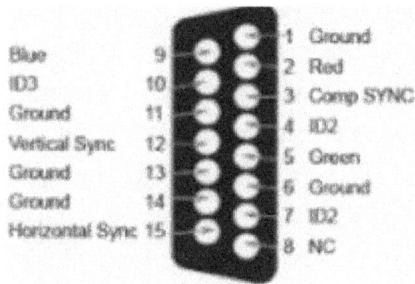

Blue	9	1 Ground
ID3	10	2 Red
Ground	11	3 Comp SYNC
Vertical Sync	12	4 ID2
Ground	13	5 Green
Ground	14	6 Ground
Horizontal Sync	15	7 ID2
		8 NC

Fig. 29 – Micro HDMI connector pin assignments
Typical Price – $5.19 - $9.06

MicroSD CARD

Purpose - Smaller version of SD memory card, built specifically for external storage in compact devices like cellphones, smartphones and Nintendo™ Switch™, devices.. MicroSD cards are also hot-pluggable and hot-swappable just like the larger SD cards.

Fig. 30 – MicroSD Card connector

Pinout - (See manufacturer's specs and the Glossary for more.)

Pin	SD	SPI
1	DAT2	X
2	CD/DAT3	CS
3	CMD	DI
4	VDD	VDD
5	CLK	SCLK
6	VSS	VSS
7	DAT0	DO
8	DAT1	X

Fig. 31 – MicroSD Card connector pin assignment

Typical Price – $11.00 - $29.99

Mini-DIN

Purpose - multi-pin electrical connector used for keyboards, mice, serial printers, modems and game controllers. Mini-DIN is similar to the larger, older DIN connector, and come with three to nine pins in seven patterns,

Graphic -

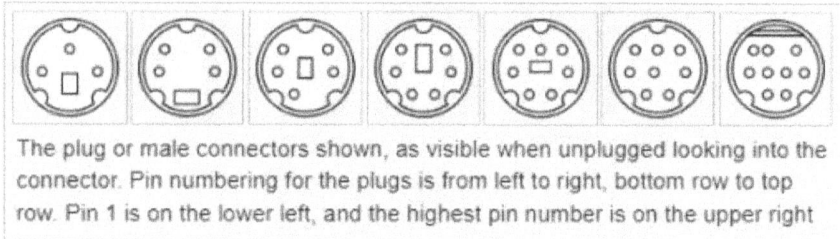

The plug or male connectors shown, as visible when unplugged looking into the connector. Pin numbering for the plugs is from left to right, bottom row to top row. Pin 1 is on the lower left, and the highest pin number is on the upper right

Fig. 32 – Mini-DIN connectors

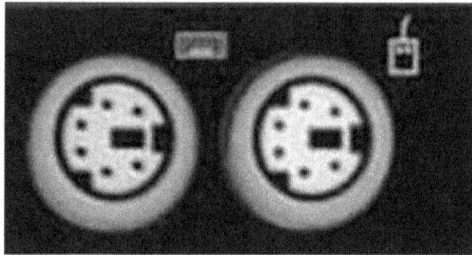

Fig. 33 – RGB keyboard and mouse connectors (for gaming)

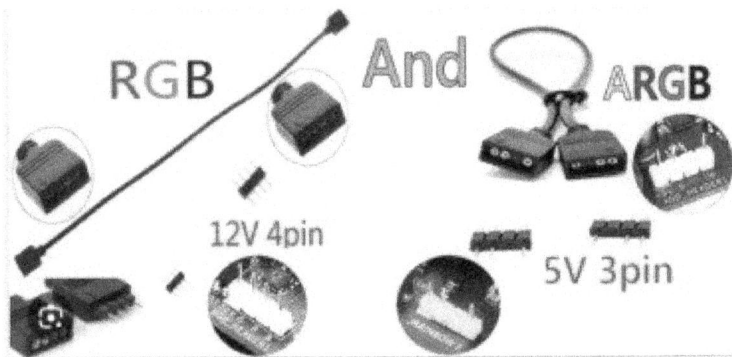

Fig. 34 – PS/2 (Personal System 2) connector: Introduced in 1985 by IBM; 6-pin DIN

Pinout - (See manufacturer's specs.)

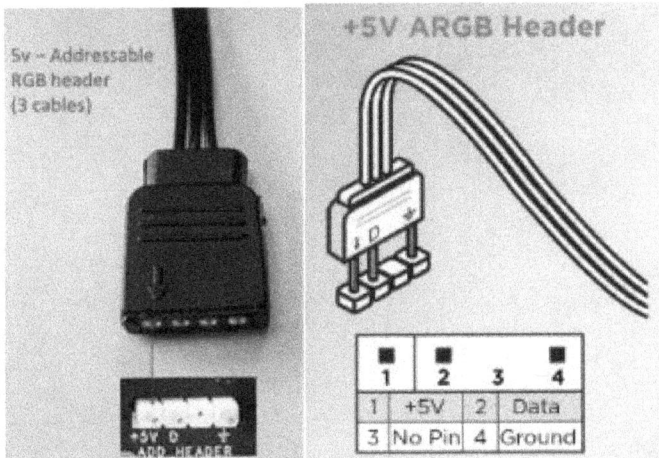

Fig. 35 – Mini DIN connector pin assignment

Typical Price – $6.95 - $12.90

Mini-HDMI (Mini High Definition Multimedia Interface)

Purpose – used to transfer uncompressed high-quality A/V digital signals between source and display. They often connect desktop computers to monitors, TVs to set-top boxes and games consoles to projectors

Mini HDMI, also known as Type-C, is a smaller version of the digital HDMI interface. The connector arrangement is slightly different from the larger Type-A connector.

Graphic –

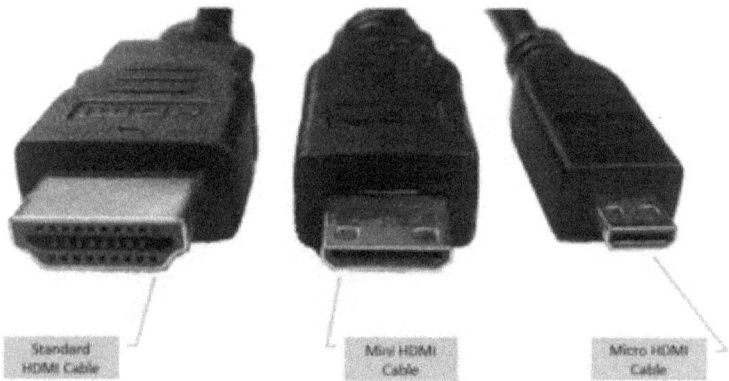

Standard HDMI Cable

Mini HDMI Cable

Micro HDMI Cable

Fig. 36 – Mini HDMI connector

Pinout -

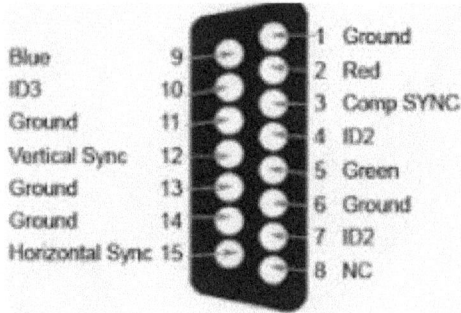

Fig. 37 – Mini HDMI connector pin assignment
Typical Price – $5.89 - $9.99

———————————————————

Nano-D

Purpose - Nano-D connectors were derived from D-subminiature and are trademarks of ITT Cannon. Their primary applications are in military and space-grade technology.

Graphic -

Fig. 38 – Nano-D connector

Pinout - (See manufacturer's specs.)

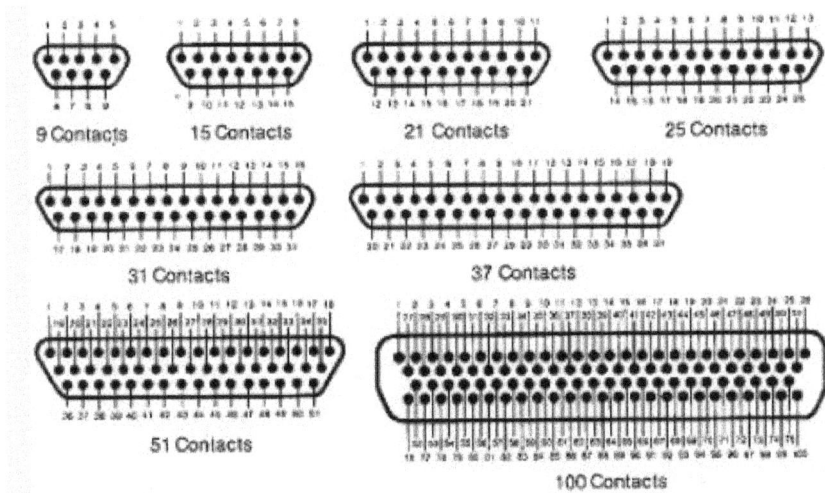

Fig. 39 – Nano-D connector pinouts

Typical Price – $18.99 - $21.25

_____

Phone Connector

Purpose – A (tip-ring-sleeve) phone connector called
an audio jack, phone plug, jack plug, stereo plug, mini-
jack, or mini-stereo. This includes the original 6.35mm
(quarter inch) jack and the more recent 3.5mm
(miniature or 1/8inch) and 2.5mm (subminiature)
jacks, both mono and stereo versions.

.Graphic -

Fig. 40 – Phone jack connectors

Pinout -

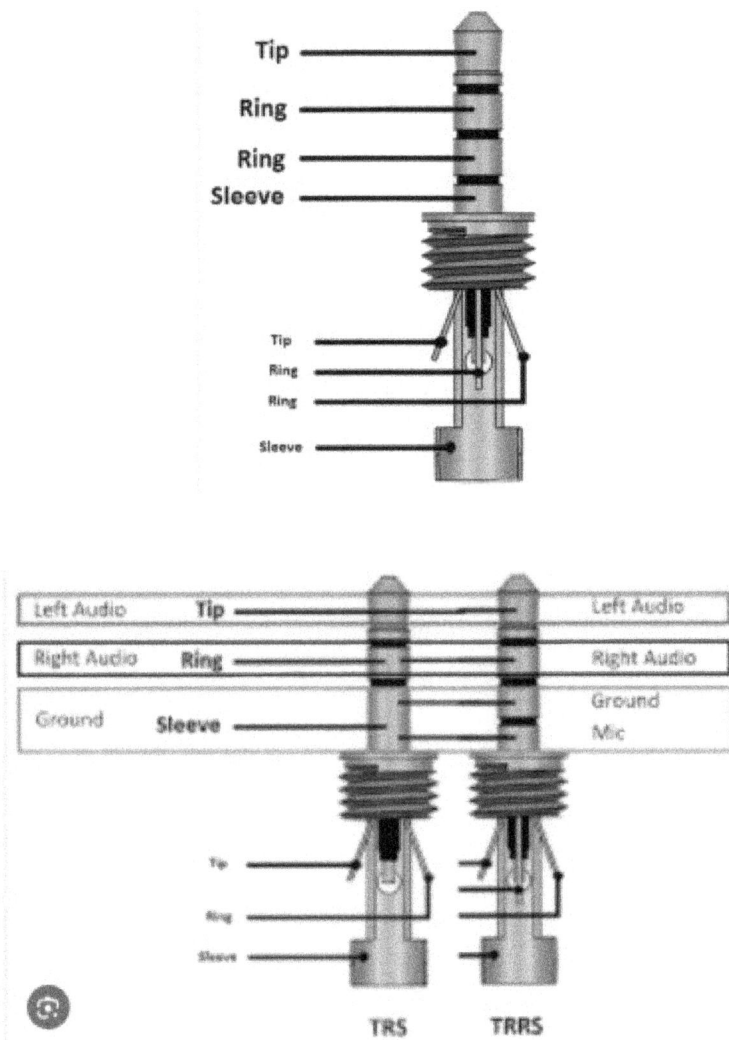

Tip
Ring
Ring
Sleeve

Tip
Ring
Ring
Sleeve

Left Audio	Tip	Left Audio
Right Audio	Ring	Right Audio
Ground	Sleeve	Ground
		Mic

Tip
Ring
Sleeve

TRS   TRRS

5mm Audio Jack

Fig. 41 – Phone jack assignments
Typical Price – $3.19 - $5.49

Radox

Purpose - a largely obsolete electrical interface used to connect solar panels together in series to form strings. Each connector consists of the housing and a contact element.

Graphic -

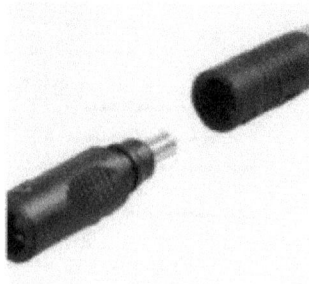

Fig. 42 – Radox connector

Pinout – A single plus or minus contact element is in each connector.

Typical Price – $7.19 - $19.65

————————————————————

RCA

Purpose – *phono* connectors or *phono plugs* used for analog or digital audio and analog video. RCA Plugs for composite video are yellow and for stereo audio are white and red.

Graphic -

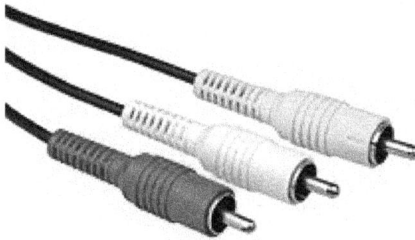

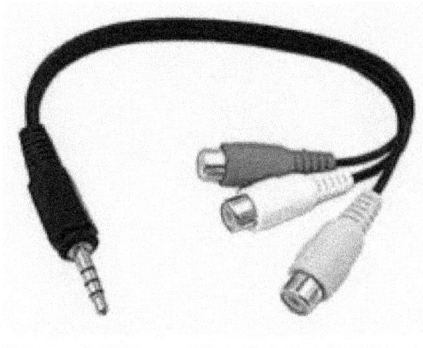

Fig. 43 – RCA connectors

Pinout –

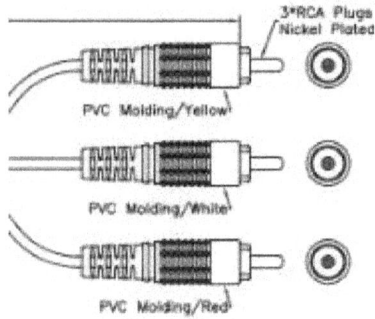

Fig. 44 – RCA jack assignments

Typical Price – $4.79 - $9.99

————————————————————

RJ11 (Registered Jack 11)

Purpose – connects a telephone to a phone line; an older version of RJ12, and the same size. The difference is that RJ11 uses four internal wires (called conductors) while the RJ12 cable uses six. RJ12 is backwards compatible with RJ11, but RJ11 will not work with RJ12. RJ11 usually has a size of 6mm. It features 6 positions and 2 or 4 pins, and is widely used in telephone systems and ADSL/VDSL modems.

Graphic -

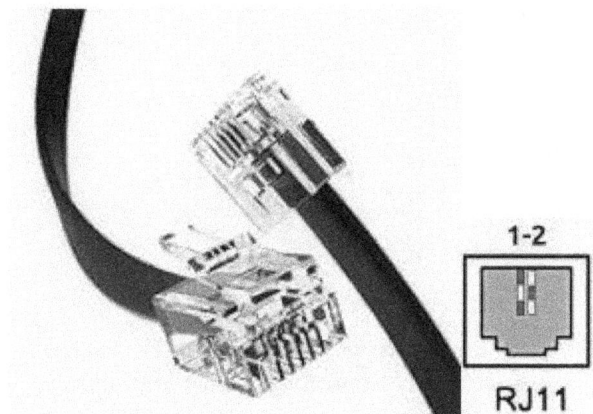

Fig. 45 – RJ11 connectors

Pinout -

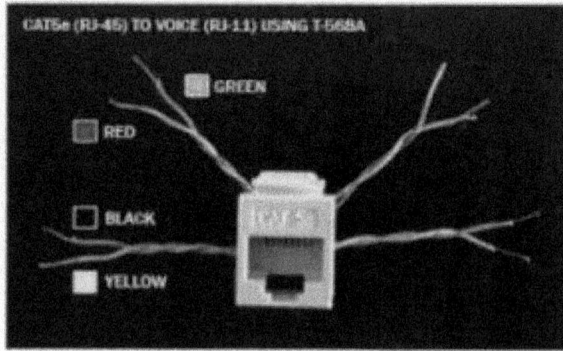

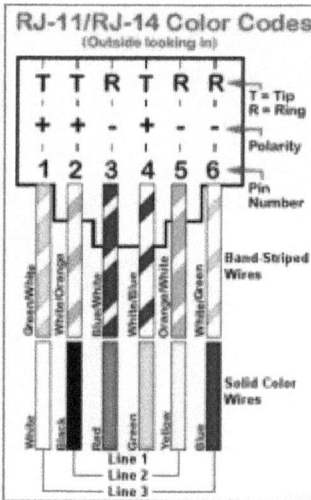

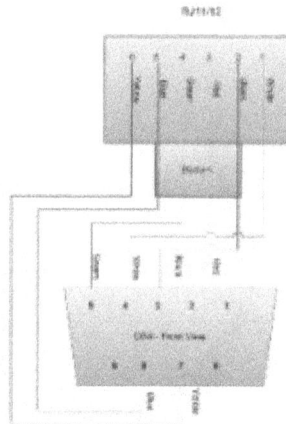

Fig. 46 – RJ11 connector pin assignments
Typical Price – $5.89 - $14.60

RJ12

Purpose - a connector for both data and voice. It can be used for telephones, switchboards, broadband, fax machines, DSL modems, point of sale cash drawers and also in printers and radio control systems.

Graphic -

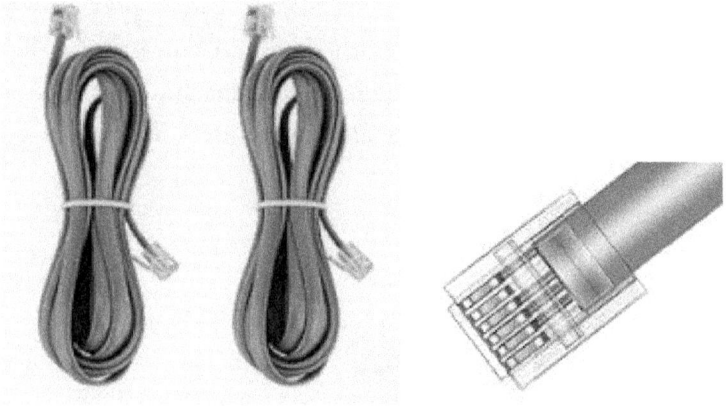

Fig. 47 – RJ12 connectors

Pinout -

please make sure that you're clear about its wiring diagram:
1–2–3–4–5–6 pin to 1–2–3–4–5–6 pin

6p6c_{plugs}

pin1 -- pin1 (white)

pin2 -- pin2 (black)

pin3 -- pin3 (red)

pin4 -- pin4 (green)

pin5 -- pin5 (yellow)

pin6 -- pin6 (blue)

Fig. 48 – RJ12 pin assignment
Typical Price – $0.14 - $2.85

RJ14

Purpose –used for crimping and terminating voice & data cables. RJ14 and RJ11 are extremely similar, but RJ14 includes an extra two pins for data transmission. RJ11 can support only two wires, but RJ14 can support four wires. This means that you must use an RJ-14 connector if you need to connect more than two telephone lines. RJ14 connectors are similar to RJ11 connectors, but they have 4 pins instead of 6. They are commonly used to connect two telephone lines and are often found in residential and small business telephone systems.

Graphic -

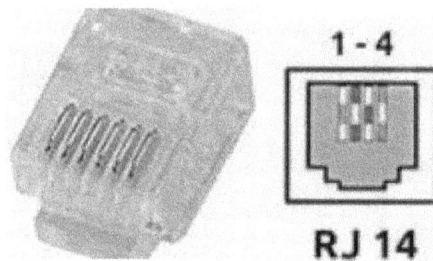

Fig. 49 – RJ14 connectors

Pinout -

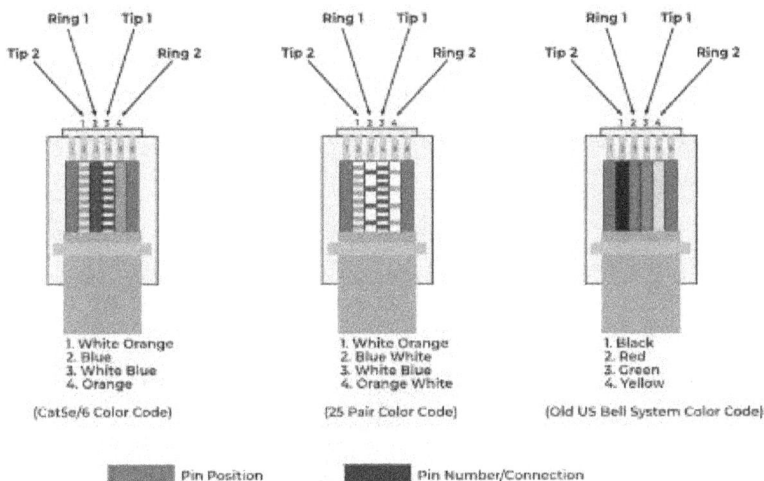

Fig. 50 – RJ14 pin assignments
Typical Price – $1.55 - $4.99

RJ45

Purpose – the standard connector for Cat5 and Cat6 cables. The cables are normally terminated using either T568A or T568B pin assignments; performance is comparable provided both ends of the cable are terminated identically.

Graphic -

Fig. 51 – RJ45 connectors

Pinout -

Pin	Description	10base-T	100Base-T	1000Base-T
1	Transmit Data+ or BiDirectional	TX+	TX+	BI_DA+
2	Transmit Data- or BiDirectional	TX-	TX-	BI_DA-
3	Receive Data+ or BiDirectional	RX+	RX+	BI_DB+
4	Not connected or BiDirectional	n/c	n/c	BI_DC+
5	Not connected or BiDirectional	n/c	n/c	BI_DC-
6	Receive Data- or BiDirectional	RX-	RX-	BI_DB-
7	Not connected or BiDirectional	n/c	n/c	BI_DD+
8	Not connected or BiDirectional	n/c	n/c	BI_DD-

1 2 3 4 5 6 7 8

T-568A

Fig. 52 – RJ45 pin assignments
Typical Price – $0.08 - $7.99

RS232 (Recommended Standard 232)

Purpose – a telecommunication interface for serial communication transmission of data. signals between a DTE device such as a computer terminal, and a DCE device, such as a modem.

Graphic -

Fig. 53 – RS232 connectors

Pinout -

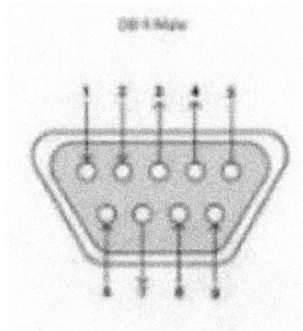

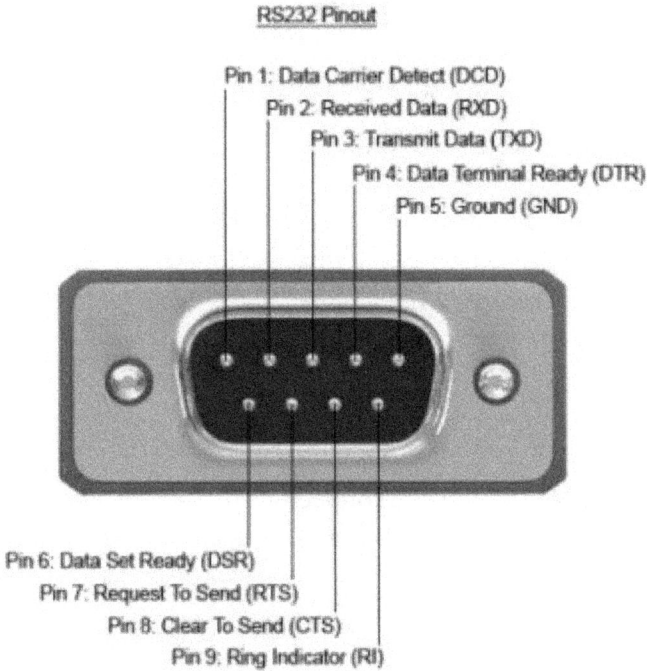

Fig. 54 – RS232 connector pin assignments
Typical Price – $4.99 - $7.96

RS422

Purpose – This connector is also known as TIA/EIA-422 to specify the electrical characteristics of a serial digital signaling circuit.

Graphic -

Fig. 55 – RS422 connector

Pinout -

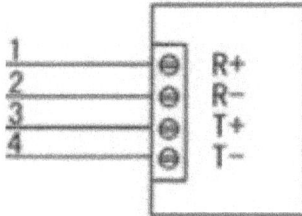

Fig. 56 – RS422 connector pin assignments

Typical Price – $16.98 - $23.98

————————————————————

SATA (Serial Advanced Technology Attachment)

Purpose – a computer bus interface that connects host bus adapters to mass storage devices such as hard disk drives, optical drives, and solid-state drives

Graphic -

Fig. 57 – SATA connectors

Pinout -

Pin #	Mating	Function
1	1st	Ground
2	2nd	A+ (transmit)
3	2nd	A– (transmit)
4	1st	Ground
5	2nd	B– (receive)
6	2nd	B+ (receive)
7	1st	Ground
—		Coding notch

Pin #	Mating	Function
—		Coding notch
1	3rd	3.3 V power
2	3rd	
3	2nd	Enter/exit Power Disable (PWDIS) mode (3.3 V power, pre-charge prior to SATA 3.3)
4	1st	
5	2nd	Ground
6	2nd	
7	2nd	5 V power, pre-charge
8	3rd	5 V power
9	3rd	
10	2nd	Ground
11	3rd	Staggered spinup / activity signal / direct head unload / vendor specific
12	1st	Ground
13	2nd	12 V power, pre-charge
14	3rd	12 V power
15	3rd	

Data connector   **Power connectors**

Fig. 58 – SATA connector pin assignments
Typical Price – $1.33 - $7.99

———————————————————

SCSI (Small Computer System Interface)

Purpose - to connect computer devices using a common interface.

Graphic -

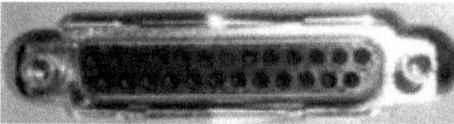

Fig. 59 – SCSI connectors

Pinout -

SCSI Connector Pinout

PIN	NAME
50	I/O
48	REQ
46	C/D
44	SEL
42	MSG
40	RST
38	ACK
36	BSY
34	NC
32	ATN
30	GROUND
28	GROUND
26	NOT USED
24	GROUND
22	GROUND
20	GROUND
18	DB (P)
16	DB (7)
14	DB (6)
12	DB (5)
10	DB (4)
8	DB (3)
6	DB (2)
4	DB (1)
2	DB (0)

PIN	NAME	PIN	NAME
1	REQ	14	GROUND
2	MSG	15	C/D
3	I/O	16	GROUND
4	RST	17	ATN
5	ACK	18	GROUND
6	BSY	19	SEL
7	GROUND	20	DB (P)
8	DB (0)	21	DB (1)
9	GROUND	22	DB (2)
10	DB (2)	23	DB (4)
11	DB (8)	24	GROUND
12	DB (6)	25	TPWR
13	DB (7)		

ALL ODD PINS, EXCEPT PIN 25, ARE GROUND.
PIN 25 IS NOT USED.

GND	20	19	GND
Rx2n	21	18	Rx1n
Rx2p	22	17	Rx1p
GND	23	16	GND
Rx4n	24	15	Rx3n
Rx4p	25	14	Rx3p
GND	26	13	GND
ModPrsL	27	12	SDA
IntL	28	11	SCL
Vcc Tx	29	10	Vcc Rx
Vcc1	30	9	ResetL
LPMode	31	8	ModSelL
GND	32	7	GND
Tx3p	33	6	Tx4p
Tx3n	34	5	Rx4n
GND	35	4	GND
Tx1p	36	3	Tx2p
Tx1n	37	2	Tx2n
GND	38	1	GND

Fig. 60 – SCSI connector pin assignments
Typical Price – $13.95 - $22.66

————————————————————

SD Card (Secure Digital card)

Purpose - a specific type of memory storage format developed by the SD Card Association. These cards come in 2GB, 4GB, 16GB, 32GB, and 64GB sizes and standard, mini and micro physical sizes. SD cards are commonly used in digital cameras, camcorders, smartphones, tablets, and other portable devices to store photos, videos, music, documents, and other data.

Graphic -

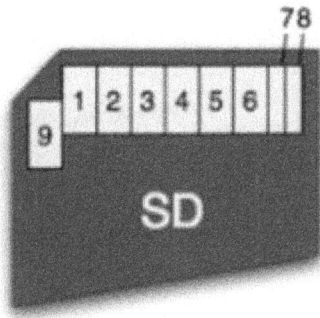

Fig. 61 – SD card

Pinout -

Pin	SD	SPI
1	CD/DAT3	CS
2	CMD	DI
3	VSS1	VSS1
4	VDD	VDD
5	CLK	SCLK
6	VSS2	VSS2
7	DAT0	DO
8	DAT1	X
9	DAT2	X

Fig. 62 – SD card pin assignments
Typical Price – $12.99 - $26.99

————————————————————

S/PDIF (Sony/Philips Digital Interface)

Purpose - a digital audio interface used in consumer audio equipment to output audio over relatively short lines of wire to interconnect components in home theaters and other digital high-fidelity systems

Graphic -

Fig. 63 – S/PDIF connectors

Pinout –

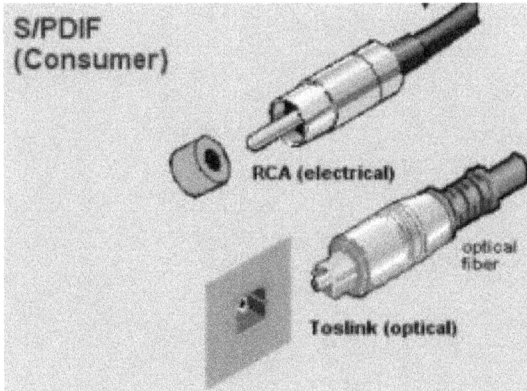

Fig. 64 – S/PDIF connector types

Typical Price – $5.69 - $11.95

T4

Purpose - a type of solar panel connector developed by Amphenol Industrial Solar Technologies. They were designed as an alternative to Universal Solar Connectors.

Graphic -

Fig. 65 – T4 connectors

Pinout – Single conductor cable for the positive voltage and a separate connector for the negative return.

Typical Price – $0.70 each - $6.79 per set

————————————————————

TOSLINK (Toshiba Link)

Purpose – a standardized optical fiber connection system.to convert electric audio signals to light that is transmitted serially through a fiber made of plastic, glass, or silica.

Graphic –

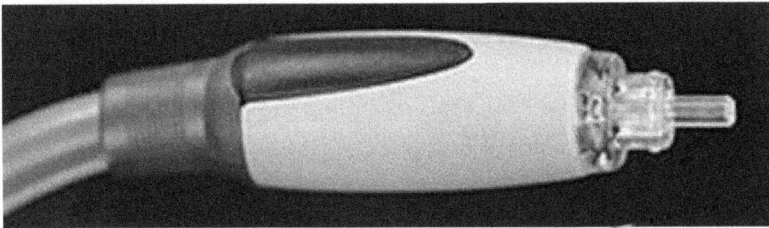

Fig. 66 – Clear TOSLINK cable with round connector

Pinout - Single conductor with one center pin

Typical Price – $5.69 - $12.79

————————————————

Tyco Solarlok

Purpose – a gender neutral power connector for solar panels, micro inverters, combiner boxes and DC optimizers to allow any two connectors to mate without needing male and female parts. Solarloks are designed to connect solar panels to the power grid for 1500V DC cable solutions.

Graphic –

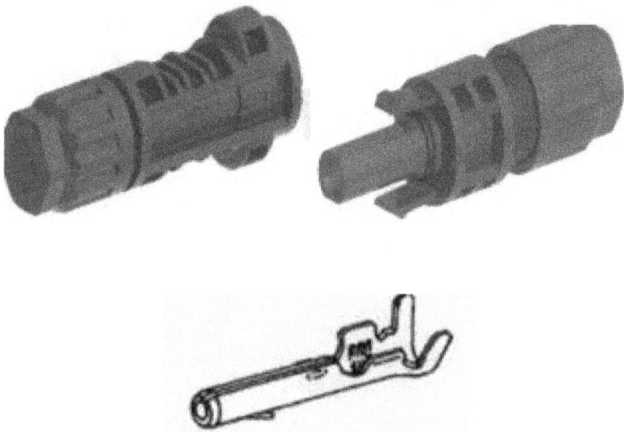

Fig. 67 – TYCO connectors

Pinout – Use two solar interface cables – one for positive and the other for negative connection.

Typical Price – $5.25 - $7.19 set

USB 1 (Universal Serial Bus version 1)

Purpose – A serial interface for keyboards, mice, joysticks, printers, and scanners that don't need faster data transfer rates than 1.5 MBps standard speed (12 MBps full speed).

Graphic -

Fig. 68 – USB1 connectors

Pinout -

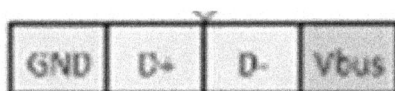

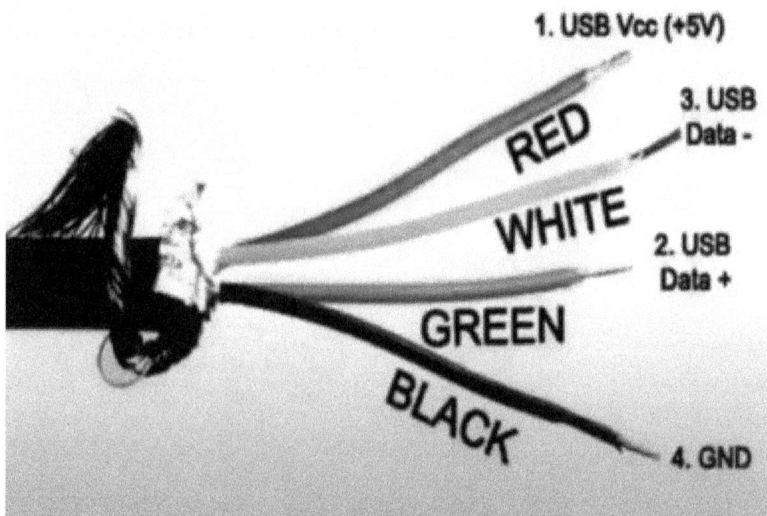

Fig. 69 – USB1 connector pin assignments
Typical Price – $1.00 - $3.99

USB 2 (Universal Serial Bus version 2)

Purpose – A serial interface for keyboards, mice, joysticks, printers, and scanners. USB 2.0 can transfer data at 480 MBps over an interface cable up to 15 meters (49 feet) long.

Graphic -

USB 2.0

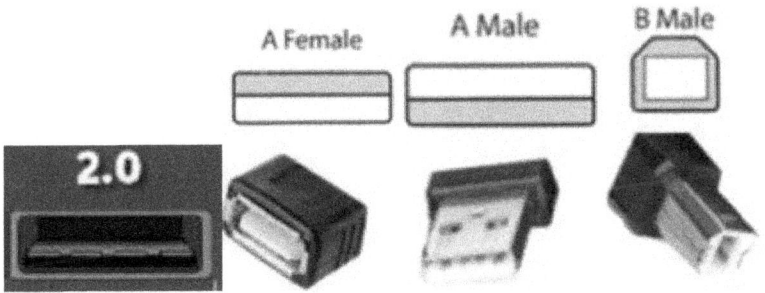

Micro B Male

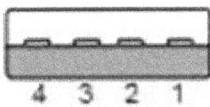

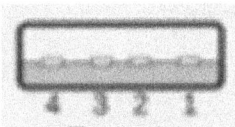

Fig. 70 – USB2 connectors

Pinout -

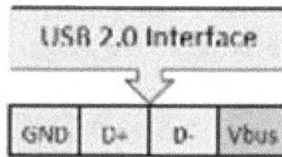

Fig. 71 – USB2 connector pin assignments

Typical Price – $1.08 - $5.39

————————————————————

USB 2a

Purpose – a serial interface for printers, digital cameras, smartphones, and MP3 players. The main difference between USB Type 2a and Type 2b is the shape, as the rounding has been altered due to the increase of the number of pins; allowing a faster data transfer.

Graphic -

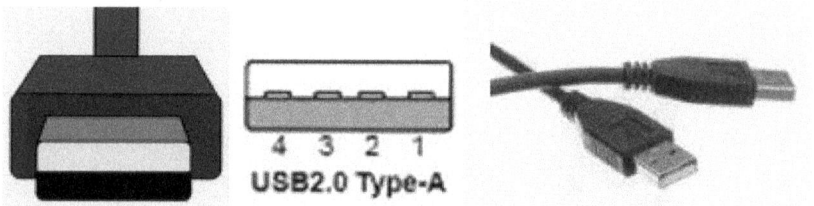

Fig. 72 – USB2 TypeA connector

Pinout -

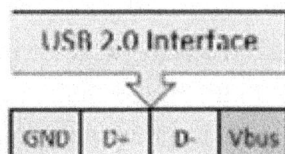

Fig. 73 – USB2a connector pin assignments
Typical Price – $2.46 - $5.39

——————————————————————

USB 3.0 (Universal Serial Bus version 3)

Purpose – A serial interface for keyboards, mice, joysticks, printers, scanners and mobile phones, tablets, laptops, and extended data cables, charging heads, mobile power supplies and other digital accessories.

Graphic -

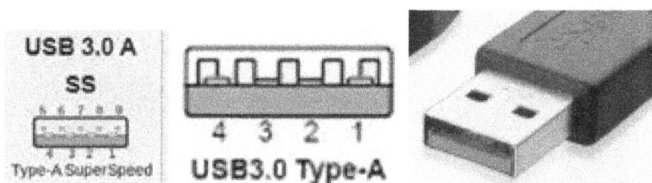

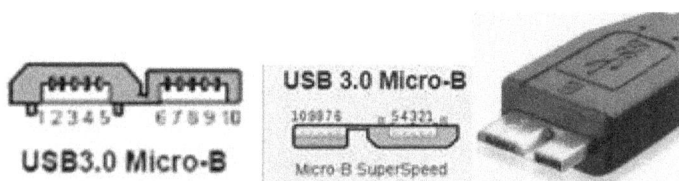

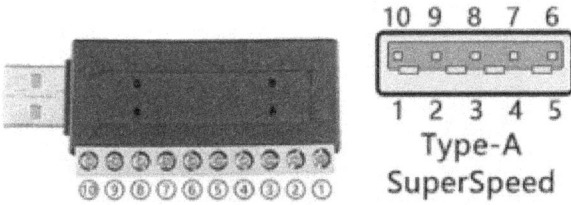

Type-A
SuperSpeed

USB 3.0/3.1/3.2

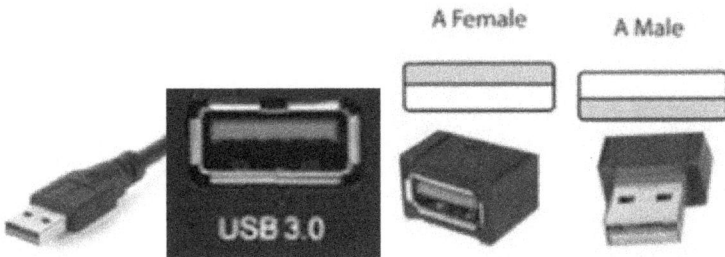

USB 3.0 SS

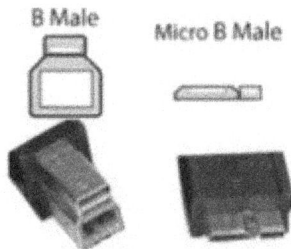

USB 3.0 SS

USB 3.0 Gen 1 Type B Standard
Fig. 74 – USB3.0 connectors

Pinout –

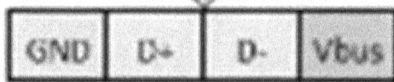

USB 3.0 Type A

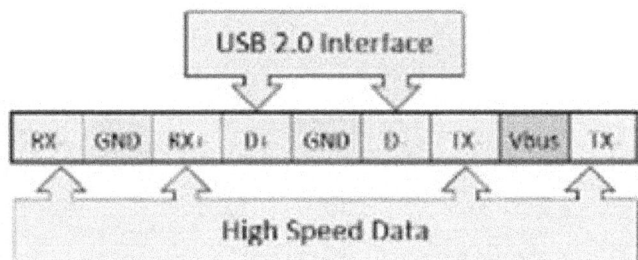

Pin number	signal (Type A)	signal (Type B)
1	VBUS	
2	D-	
3	D+	
4	GND	
5	StdA_SSTX-	
6	StdA SSTX+	
7	GND	
8	StdA _SSRX-	
9	StdA_SSRX+	
10	SHELL	

USB 3.0 Type A   **USB 3.0 A SS**

Connector Pins	Name	Cable Color	Function
1	VCC	Red	+5V DC
2	D-	White	Data -
3	D+	Green	Data +
4	GND	Black	Ground
5	StdB_SSRX-	Blue	SuperSpeed transmit -
6	StdB_SSRX+	Yellow	SuperSpeed transmit +
7	GND_Drain	N/A	Ground signal return
8	StdB_SSTX-	Purple	SuperSpeed receive -
9	StdB_SSTX+	Orange	SuperSpeed receive +

USB 3.0 Type B Super Speed (SS)
Fig. 75 – USB 3.0 connector pin assignments
Typical Price – $1.29 - $9.99

————————————————————

USB 3.1 USB 3.2 USB 3.4 USB 4 C

Purpose - serial interfaces used in mobile phones, tablets, laptops, and extended data cables, charging heads, mobile power supplies and other digital accessories. USB 3.1 has a data transfer rate of 5 GBps. USB 3.2 Type A Superspeed (SS) has a transfer speed of 10 GBps, USB 3.4 Type B Superspeed (SS) has a transfer speed of 20 MBps and USB 4 C has a transfer speed of 40 GBps.

Graphic -

Fig. 76 – USB 3.1, 3.2. 3.4, and 4 C connectors

Pinout -

1	2	3	4
VBUS (+)	D-	D+	GND
RED	WHITE	GREEN	BLAKC

Fig. 77 – USB 3.1, 3.2. 3.4, 4 C connector pinouts

Typical Price – 3.1a = $7.19

3.2a = $5.99
3.4b = $6.99
4C = $10.99

USB Mini

Purpose - a small interface for printers, digital cameras, smartphones, and MP3 players.

Graphic -

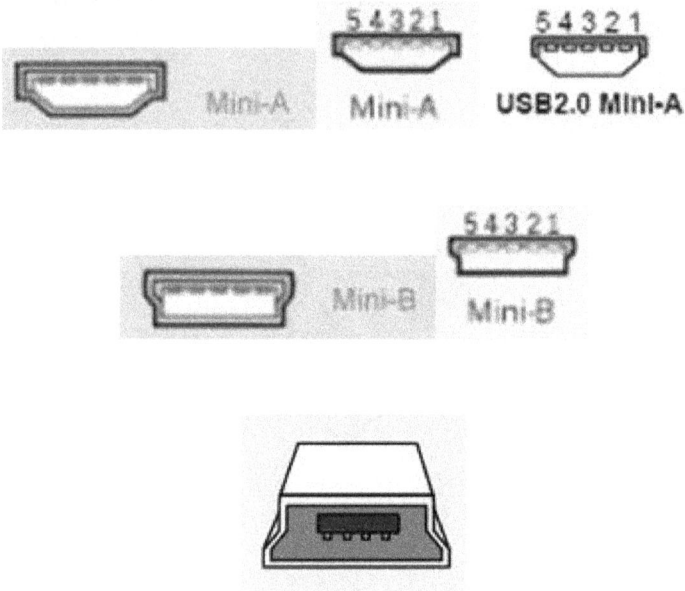

USB B Mini

Fig. 78 – USB.Mini connectors

Pinout – (5 pins)

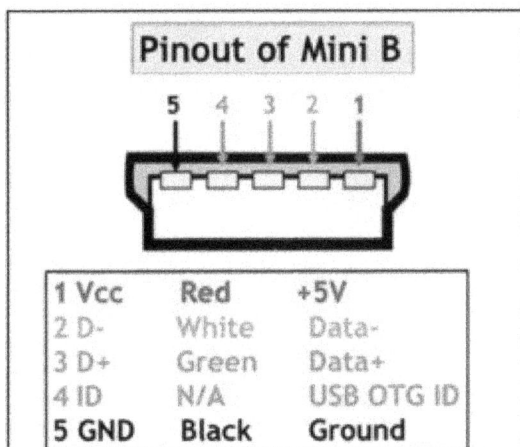

Fig. 79 – Mini-USB Type B connector pin assignments
Typical Price – $5.20 - $8.99

USB Micro

Purpose - a miniaturized version of the USB interface developed for connecting compact and mobile devices, such as smartphones, MP3 players, Global Positioning System devices, printers and digital cameras. The micro-USB connector was introduced in January 2007. It has been superseded by USB Type C.

Graphic -

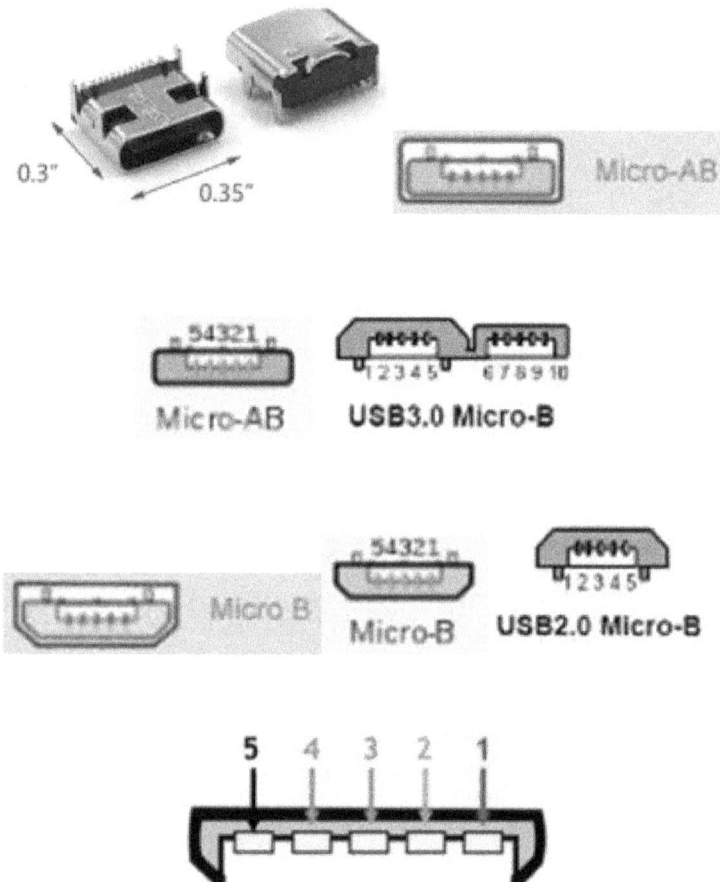

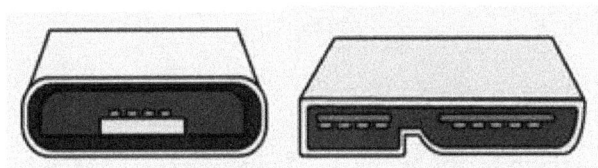

2.0 3.0

Fig. 80 – USB.Micro connectors

Pinout - (5 or 10 pins)

1 Vcc	Red	+5V
2 D-	White	Data-
3 D+	Green	Data+
4 ID	N/A	USB OTG ID
5 GND	Black	Ground

USB 2.0 Micro Type B

Connector Pins	Name	Cable Color	Function
1	VCC	Red	+5V DC
2	D-	White	Data -
3	D+	Green	Data +
4	GND	Black	Ground
5	StdB_SSRX-	Blue	SuperSpeed transmit -
6	StdB_SSRX+	Yellow	SuperSpeed transmit +
7	GND_Drain	N/A	Ground signal return
8	StdB_SSTX-	Purple	SuperSpeed receive -
9	StdB_SSTX+	Orange	SuperSpeed receive +

USB 3.0 Type B Super Speed

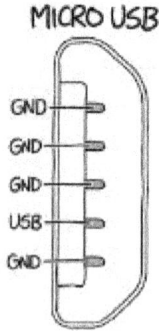

Fig. 81 – USB.Micro connector pin assignments
Typical Price – $4.39 - $6.99

———————————————————

USB Type A

Purpose – a serial interface for printers, digital cameras, smartphones, and MP3 players. The cable has a wide USB Type A at one end. The connector is not rotationally symmetrical and both ends of the cable are different, corresponding to a different type of port. USB Type A is compatible with: USB 1.1 Type A, USB 2.0 Type A and USB 3.0.

Graphic -

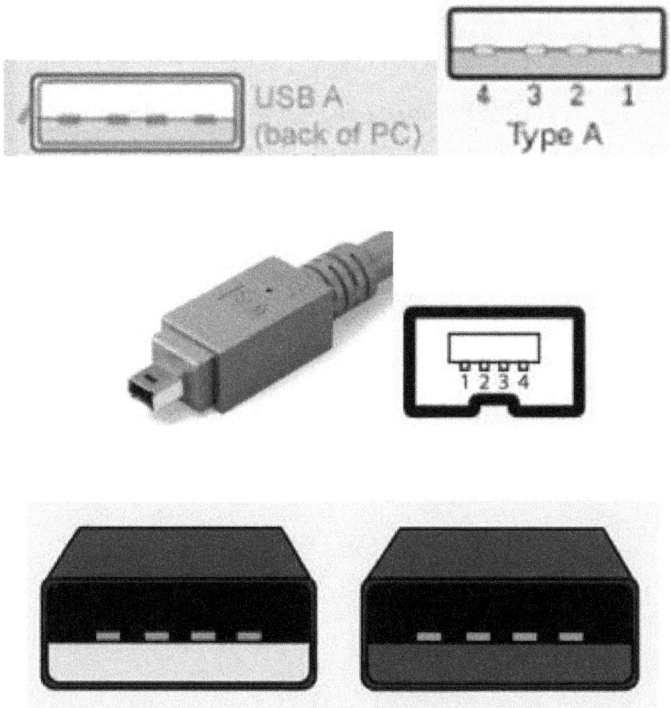

Fig. 82 – USB.Type A connectors

Pinout - (4 pins) The Type-A, connector contains four pins: two data pins (D+ and D-) and two power pins (VCC and GND).

If you were to open up a USB cable, you would notice 4 different wire colors: white and green, which carry data, and red and black, which are used for power – red carries +5 volts and acts as the positive wire, while black is the negative wire, otherwise known as the ground wire.

Pin	Name	Cable color	Description
1	VCC	Red	+5 VDC
2	D-	White	Data -
3	D+	Green	Data +
4	GND	Black	Ground

Fig. 83 – USB.Type A connector pin assignment
Typical Price – $1.08 - $1.49

————————————————————

USB Type B

Purpose – a serial interface for printers, digital cameras, scanners, smartphones, and MP3 players.

Graphic -

2.0

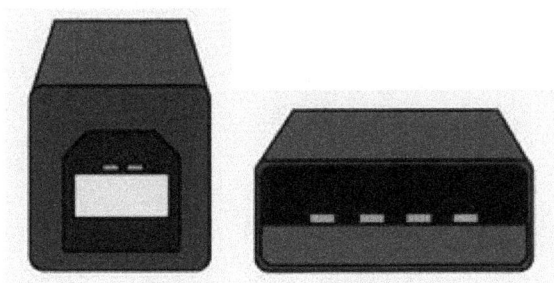

2.0   3.0

Fig. 84– USB.Type B connectors

Pinout – (4 pins)

Pin	Name	Cable color	Description
1	VCC	Red	+5 VDC
2	D-	White	Data -
3	D+	Green	Data +
4	GND	Black	Ground

Fig. 85– USB.Type B connector pin assignments
Typical Price – $0.79 - $4.50

———————————————————

USB Type C

Purpose – a serial interface for printers, digital cameras, smartphones, small mobile phones, tablets, MP3 players and large visual displays.

Graphic -

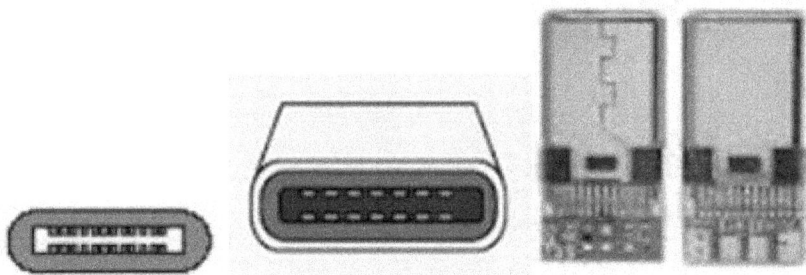

Fig. 86– USB.Type C connectors

Pinout – (12 pins x 2) A lot of pins in a tiny connector.

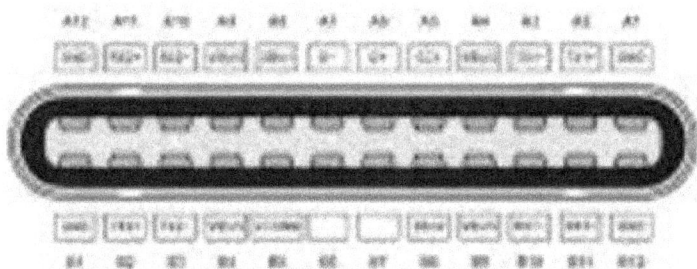

USB-C male

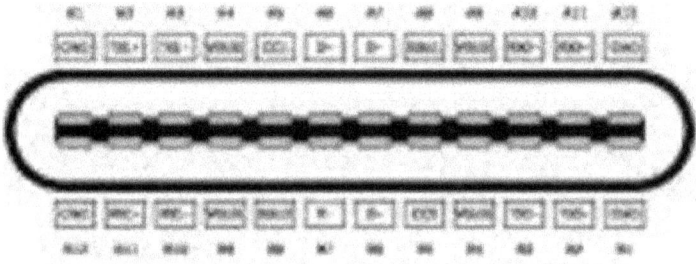

USB-C female

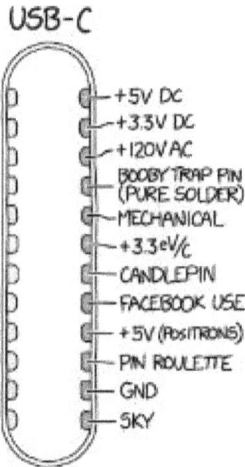

Fig. 87– USB.Type C connector pin assignments
Typical Price – $8.99 - $12.99

VGA (Video Graphics Array)

Purpose - the first display connection standard for the IBM PS/2 personal computer, The trapezoidal-shaped analog interface worked with the old CRT displays and it was widely used. Today, an array of vintage devices such as home players, projectors and TVs are still equipped with VGA ports. It's the ubiquitous standard for displaying information.

Graphic -

Fig. 88– VGA connectors

Pinout –

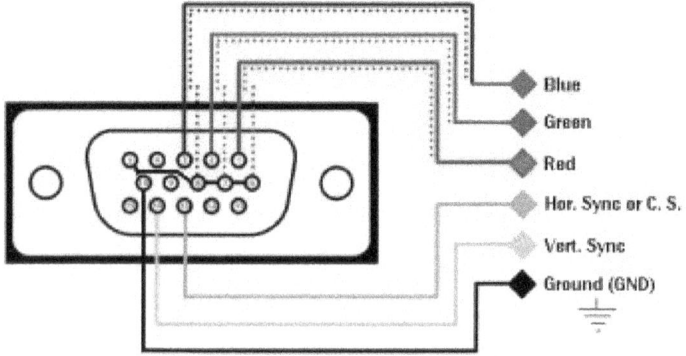

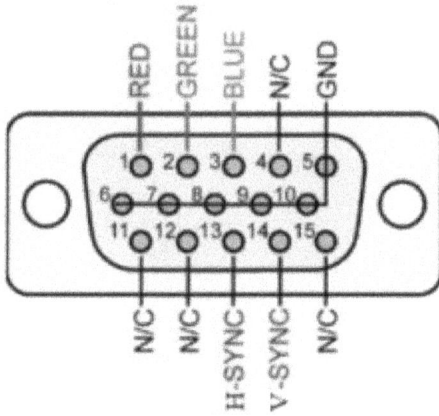

Fig. 89– VGA connector pin assignments
Typical Price – $4.32 - $9.99

———————————————————

VIVO (Video-In-Video-Out)

Purpose - a graphics card port that enables some video cards to have bidirectional (input and output) video transfer through a mini-DIN, usually of the 9-pin variety, and a specialized splitter cable (which can sometimes also transfer sound); found predominantly on high end ATI video cards, although a few high end NVIDIA video cards also have this port; typically supports Composite, S-Video and Component Video as outputs, and Composite and S-Video as inputs.

Some practical uses of VIVO include displaying multimedia stored on a computer on a TV, and being able to connect a DVD player or video game console to a computer while continuing to allow viewing via a TV monitor. VIVO itself, however, cannot decode broadcast signals from any source, and so, like HDTV sets without tuners and composite video monitors, additional equipment is required to be able to show broadcast TV programs.

Graphic -

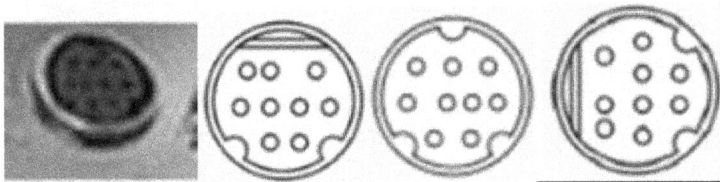

VIVO

A 6-connector VIVO splitter cable.
S-Video In, Component P out, Component P out, Component Y out;
Composite out, Composite in and S-Video Out
Fig. 90– Vivo VGA connectors

Pinout -

9-Pin DIN Connector	Pin Assignments and Connector Descriptions	
	Pin Number	Description
	1	5 V (Fused)
	2	GND
	3	Reserved
	4	Reserved
	5	Reserved
	6	PFI 1
	7	Reserved
	8	Reserved
	9	PFI 0

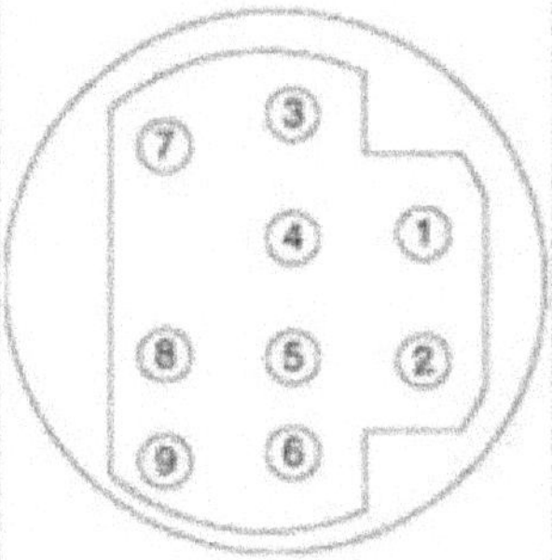

Fig. 91– VGA connector pin assignments
Typical Price – $6.92

XLR3

Purpose – a 3-pin plug (also known as *Cannon plug*) used to balance analog or digital with a balanced line. XLR3 connectors and sockets are used mostly in professional audio and video electronics cabling applications.

Graphic

XLR3 cable connectors, female on left and male on right
Fig. 92– XLR3 connectors

Pinout

RTS TW 2-wire
XLR pin-out

1. Ground

2. DC power (30V)
   Duplex audio 1

3. Duplex audio 2

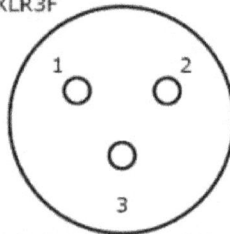

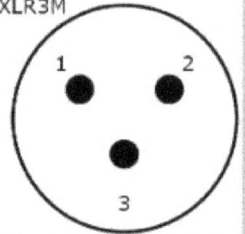

Fig. 93– XLR3 connector pin assignments
Typical Price – $1.16 - $9.99

XLR4

Purpose - a 4-pin XLR connector used for intercom headsets. Two pins are used for the mono headphone signal and two pins are for the unbalanced microphone signal.

Graphic -

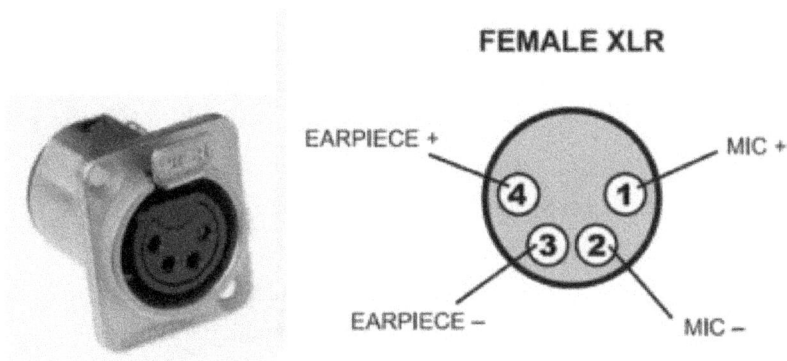

Fig. 94– XLR4 connector

Pinout – (Also see manufacturer's specs)

Four Pin Intercom Headset

Pin 1 – microphone ground

Pin 2 – microphone input

Pin 3 – headphone ground

Pin 4 – headphone signal output

Typical Price – $3.00 - $8.99

======================================

CONNECTOR ADAPTERS

The following adapters are described next.

DB9 to DB25 Serial Adapter

DB15 VGA to 15-pin Breakout Board Adapter

DB25 to RS232 Adapter

HDMI Type A or Type C to M12 Adapter

Micro-USB to HDMI Adapter

RJ45 to Cat 5/6/7

Solar 1-to-4 Branch Connector

Solar Single to Parallel Y Connector

USB 2.0 to DB9-Sub

USB A to USB B Printer Cable

USB Serial TTL to Audio Jack

USB Standard to USB Type B

USB to Serial RS232 DB25 Adapter

USB Type C to Open Wire End

————————————————————

DB9 to DB25 Adapter

$7.75 $16.99

Fig. 95 – DB9 to DB25 Adapter cable

There are many DB9-DB25 adapters or converters for interfacing DB9 and DB25 devices.

DB15 VGA to 15-Pin Breakout Board Adapter

$14.99
Fig. 96 – DB15 VGA to 15-pin terminal block

———————————————————

DB25 to RS232 ADAPTER

$4.95 - $17.90
Fig. 97 – DB25 to RS232 Adapter cable

———————————————————

HDMI Type A or Type C to M12

$59.79
Fig.98 – HDMI Type A or C to M12 Adapter cable

———————————————————————

MICRO USB to HDMI

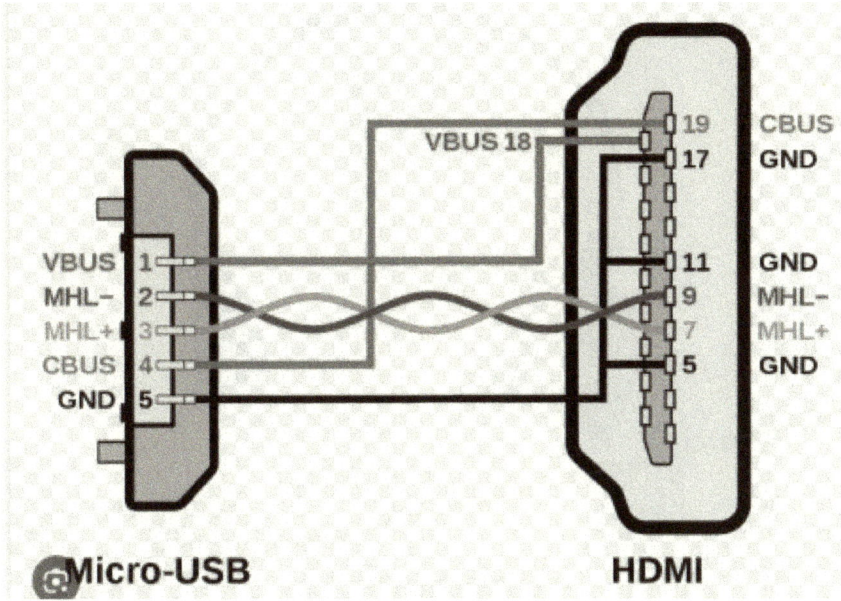

$9.73
Fig. 99 – Micro USB to HDMI Adapter

—————————————————————

RJ45 to CAT 5/6/7

Wire diagram

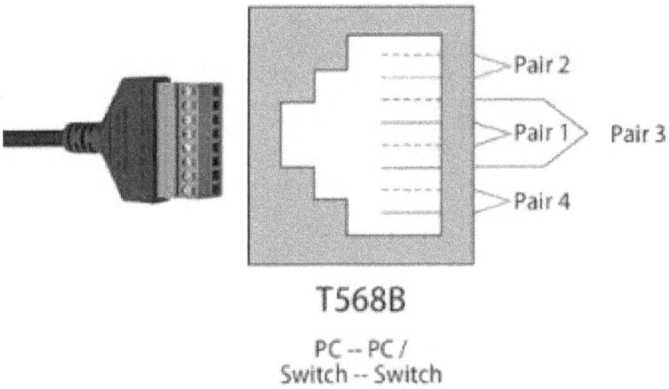

T568B

PC -- PC /
Switch -- Switch

$8.98
Fig. 100 – RJ45 to Cat 5/6/7 Adapter cable

Solar 1-to-4 Branch Connector
For solar panel parallel interface

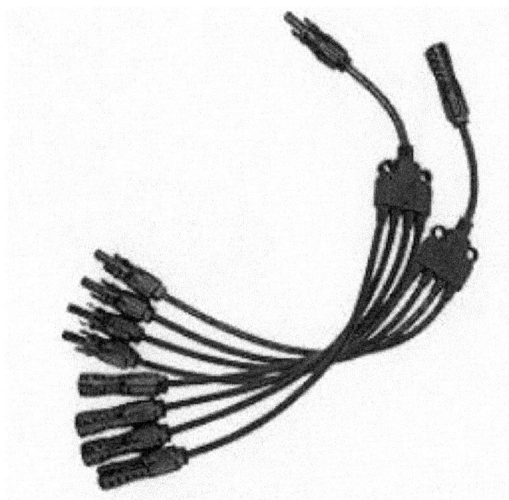

$16.99
Fig. 101 – Solar 1-to-4 branch connector

—————————————————————————

Solar Single to Parallel Y Connector

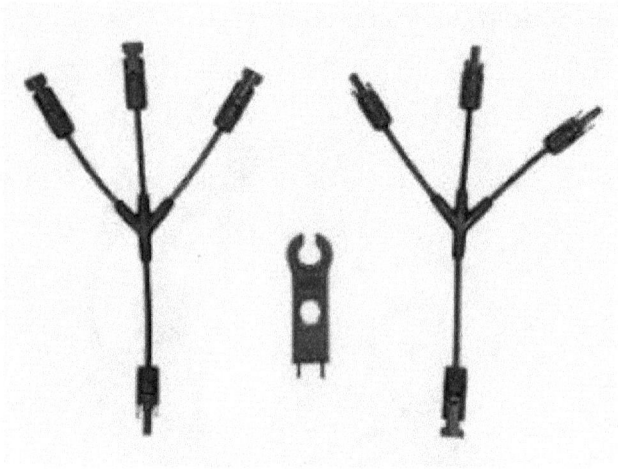

$16.99
Fig. 102 – Solar Single to Parallel Y connector

USB 2.0 to DB9 D-Sub Adapter

$22.90
Fig. 103 – USB 2.0 to DB9 D-Sub Adapter

Null Modem (Cross-Wired) RS232 serial adapter corrects DTE/DCE conflicts without requiring additional adapters or cables. Compatible with laptops, PCs and modems.

DB9 Pinouts:

2-TXD(yellow),

3-RXD(orange),

5-GND(GND),

7-CTS(green),

8-RTS(brown),

1/4/6/9-Not Connected

———————————————————

USB A to USB B Printer Cable

DataPro

$4.52-$9.99

Fig. 104 – USB Type A to USB Type B printer cable

The same USB A/B cable can be used on any scanner, printer, or other peripheral. The USB type 'A' connector is a flattened rectangle that plugs into downstream port sockets on the USB hub or USB host. The USB-B square-ish connector has two beveled corners and plugs into upstream sockets on devices and hubs.

The USB to parallel adapter is a popular solution to connecting to a printer other than to a multi-function printer with built-in scanner and fax,

USB Serial TTL to Audio Jack

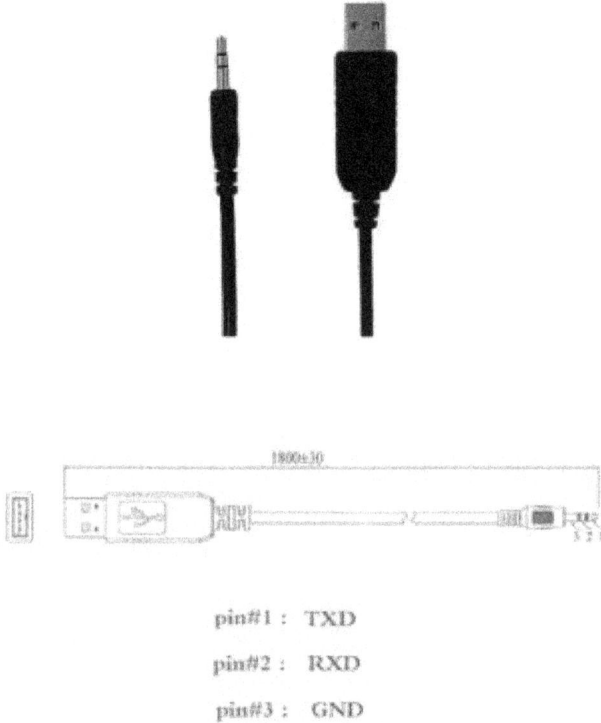

pin#1 :   TXD

pin#2 :   RXD

pin#3 :   GND

$15.00-$36.90

Fig. 105 – USB Serial RS232 to a 3.5mm Audio Jack

This USB serial TTL 3.3V cable is not terminated and has a 3.5mm audio jack connector which provides access to the RS232 TX, RX and GND signals.

Cable pinout:

1. TIP-TXD
2. RING-RXD
3. SLEEVE-GND Cable length: 6FT

————————————————————

USB Standard to USB Type B Printer Adapter

$7.49 $5.49- $9.99

Fig. 106 – USB Standard to USB Type B adapter cable
Power pins power devices, whereas data pins convey data. Printers, scanners, and other power-hungry equipment use Type-B connectors.

It contains five pins: two data pins, two power pins and one ground pin. The Type-B connector contains a ground pin and data and power pins like the Type-A connector.

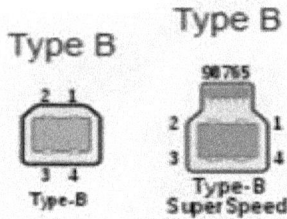

Fig. 107 – Type B connector

Type B connectors clarified which end of the cable should hook up to the host device and which to the peripheral. Type B connectors also eliminated the possibility of connecting two host computers to each other.

Here are a few updates in Type B technology:

- Each successive generation has come with increased data transfer rates.

- Versions 1.1 and 2.0 maintained the same form factor, but USB 3.0 changed the shape and introduced a second variety called Powered-B.

- Older Type B plugs are compatible with 3.0 receptacles, but 3.0 plugs are not backward compatible with older generation receptacles.

————————————————————————

USB to SERIAL RS232 DB25 ADAPTER

$12.99 - $26.99
Fig.108 – USB to Serial RS232 DB25 adapter cable

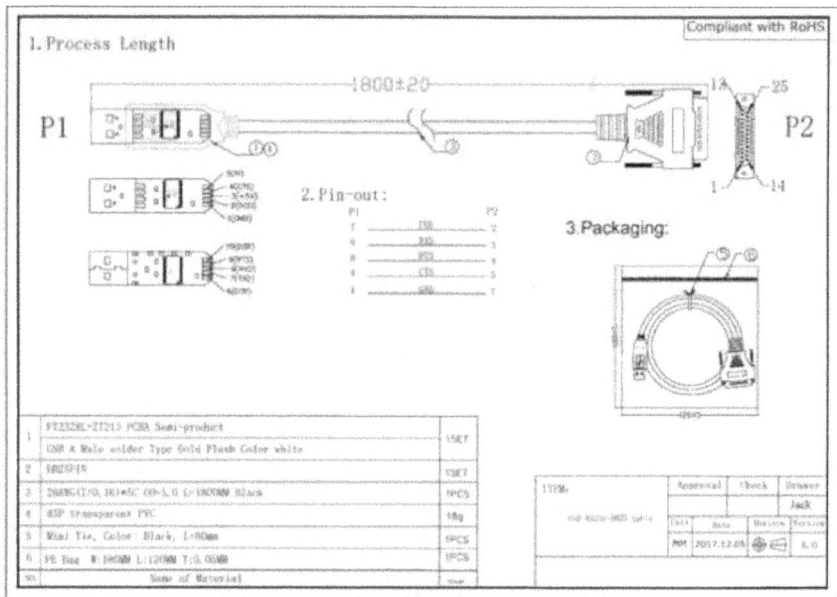

Fig. 109 – USB to RS232 adapter

Brand	AYAGROUP
Connector Type	USB Type A
Cable Type	USB
Compatible Devices	Server, Personal Computer, Printer
Color	Black

This is NOT a printer cable. This straight-thru cable converts any USB port into an RS232 connector on your computer

USB 2.0 AM			DB9/M PCB
GND	1	black	1
D+	2	green	2
D-	3	white	3
VCC	4	red	4
SHELL			SHELL

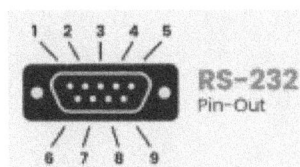

RS-232
Pin-Out

Pole	Data Type	Input / Output
1	Data Carrier	Detect (DCD)
2	Receive Data	Receive (RXD)
3	Transmit	Data (TxD)
4	Data Terminal	Ready (DTR)
5	GND	Ground Wire
6	Data Set	Ready (DSR)
7	Request!	Send (RTS)
8	Clear	Send (CTS)
9	Ringing	Indicator (RI)

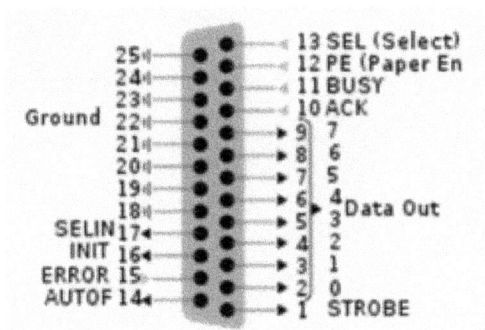

```
                          13 SEL (Select)
            25            12 PE (Paper En
            24            11 BUSY
            23            10 ACK
   Ground   22             9  7
            21             8  6
            20             7  5
            19             6  4
            18             5  3 Data Out
     SELIN 17              4  2
      INIT 16              3  1
    ERROR 15              2  0
    AUTOF 14              1  STROBE
```

DB25 Pin Assignments

1 - Strobe out		
2 - 0 out	Data Out	
3 - 1 out	Data Out	
4 - 2 out	Data Out	
0 - 3 out	Data Out	
6 - 4 out	Data Out	
7 - 5 out	Data Out	
8 - 6 out	Data Out	
9 - 7 out	Data Out	
10 - ACK in		
11 - BUSY in		
12 - PE in	Paper En	
13 - SEL in	Select	
14 - AUTOF out		
15 - ERROR in		
16 - INIT out		
17 - SELIN in		
18 – not connected		
19 – not connected		
20 – not connected		
21 – not connected		
22 = GND in	Signal Ground	
23 – not connected		
24 – not connected		
25 – not connected		

Use this cable to directly connect to a device with a mating DB-25 Female connector

USB-C 2..0 to RS-232 - $40.29

———————————————————————

USB Type C to Bare Open Wire End

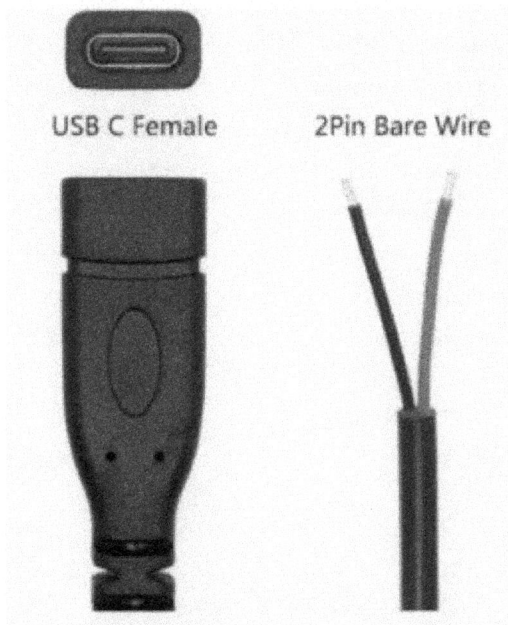

USB C Female   2Pin Bare Wire

$7.60 - $9.99
Fig. 110 – USB Type C to bare wire
<back>

POWER ADAPTERS

These adapters convert 115V AC electricity to the DC voltage and current required by a computer. When I researched this subject, I found multiple products related to power adapters.

One thing that really frustrates users is the amount of power supply adapters available these days. Many office floors are littered with adapters for routers, printers, laptops, displays, mobiles and more. It would be nice to have fewer and smaller electric plugs.

The power connectors on a PC are usually one of three shapes: the cloverleaf, figure of 8, or an IEC cord

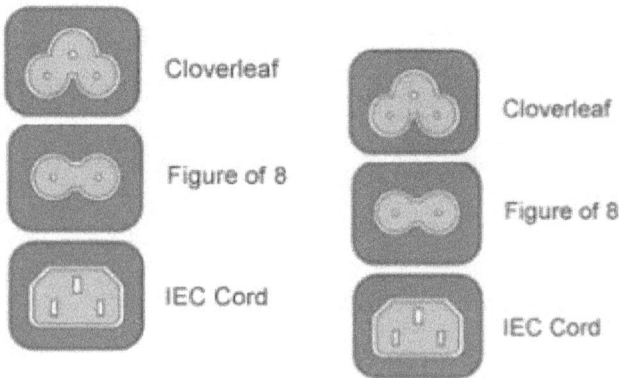

Cloverleaf

Figure of 8

IEC Cord

Cloverleaf

Figure of 8

IEC Cord

Fig. 111 – The three shapes of personal computer power connectors

Fig. 112 –Power adapters sold today

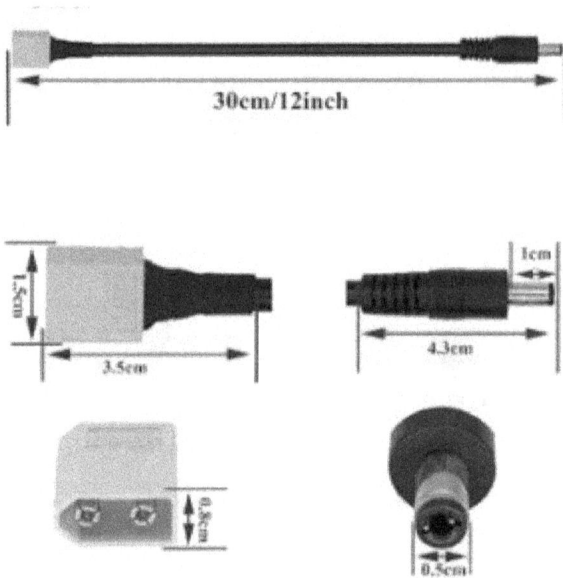

DC 2.5mm plug

Fig. 113 – Power adapter cable

AC to DC power adapters are usually provided with various plugs to accommodate the many types of receptacles for specific computers.

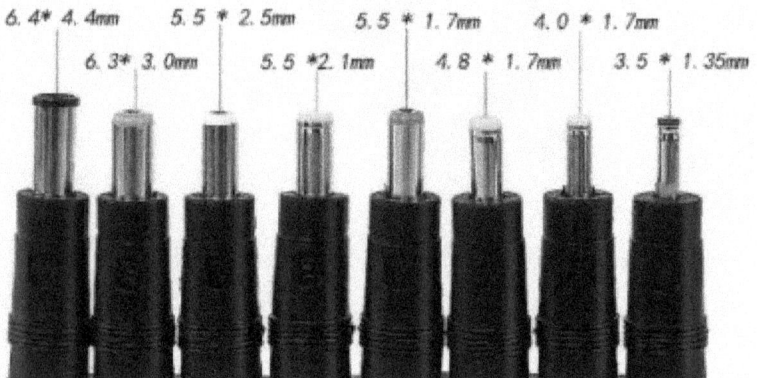

Fig. 114 – Power adapter plugs

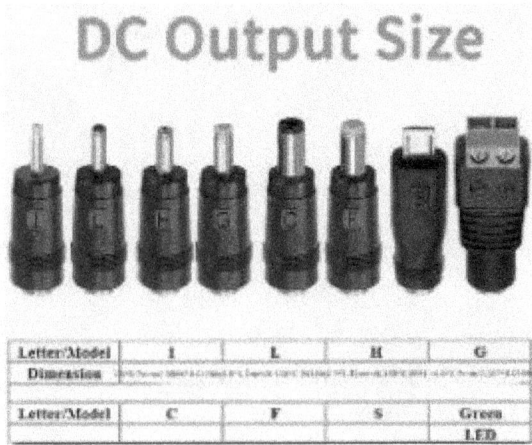

DC Output Size

Letter/Model	I	L	H	G
Dimension				
Letter/Model	C	F	S	Green LED

Fig. 115 – Power adapter plugs

Power adapters are compatible with devices of different jack plug sizes including 6.3mm, 6.0mm, 5.5mm, 4.8mm, 4.0mm, 3.5mm, 2.5mm, 2.1mm, 1.7mm, and 1.35mm.

The 5.5x2.1mm jack plug is a common size used in many laptops, making it a practical and convenient choice for those who need to power their devices on the go.

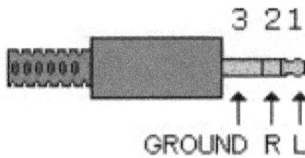

Fig. 116 – Power adapter plug

To check the ac adapter, do the following:
1. Unplug the ac adapter cable from the computer.
2. Measure the output voltage at the plug of the ac adapter cable. See the following illustration:

Pin	Voltage (V dc)
1	+20
2	0
3	Ground

(20V)

   Note: Output voltage across pin 2 of the ac power adapter might differ from the one you are servicing.
3. If the voltage is not correct, replace the ac adapter.
4. If the voltage is acceptable, replace the system board.

Fig. 117 – Power adapter pin assignment

Detachable plugs make the connection task easier.

17 Detachable Plugs

17 in 1 laptop charger, more choice and tidy for your life.

M3
16V 0-5.63A 6.5*4.5*1.35mm
For SONY FUJITSU Laptops

M4
18.5V 0-4.87A 4.8*1.7mm
For HP Laptops

M5
19V 0-4.74A 5.5*2.5mm
For TOSHIBA ASUS Laptops

M6
19V 0-4.74A 5.0*3.0mm with pin
For SAMSUNG Laptops

M8
19.5V 0-4.62A 6.5*4.4mm with pin
For SONY Laptops

M9
19.5V 0-4.62A 7.4*5.0mm with pin
For DELL Laptops

M11
20V 0-4.5A 7.9*5.4mm with pin
For LENOVO IBM Laptops

M12
18.5V 0-4.87A 7.4*5.0mm
For HP Laptops

M13
19V 0-4.74A 4.0*1.7mm
For TOSHIBA LENOVO HP DELL Laptops

M18
19V 0-4.74A 3.0*1.0mm
For ACER SAMSUNG ASUS Laptops

M19
19V 0-4.74A 4.0*1.35mm
For ASUS Laptops

M20
19V 0-4.74A 5.5*1.7mm
For ACER GATEWAY Laptops

M21
19.5V 0-4.62A 4.5*3.0mm with pin
For HP Laptops

M22
19.5V 0-4.62A 4.5*3.0mm with pin
For DELL Laptops

M27
20V 0-4.5A 11*5.0mm Square tip
For LENOVO Laptops

M31
12V 0-1A 2A 3A
For Gateway Laptops

M32
19V 0-3.15A
For Gateway Laptops

Fig. 118– Detachable plugs

And they have various voltage capabilities depending on the computer.

Fig. 119– Voltages handled

This completes the overview of connectors, sockets and plugs. May power and solid connections be good for you as you move forward in understanding and using technology.

================================

SUMMARY

This book described electronic connectors and how they relate to you and your computer. Manufacturers designed and built a wide range of connectors. Industry-government groups are trying to even out this complicated and often complex connector market and come up with standards that enable companies to provide easy-to-design solutions.

If you can access the input/output ports on a computer, you can create your own applications and ways to connect. For example, besides single, dedicated outputs, you can use ASCII to send codes that control devices.

The idea is to use the existing connector sockets on the computer or other electronic device with a plug that has open-ended stripped wires on the load end. You can use crimped connections to attach your custom output device or circuit to the computer power source. Making your own application is fun and useful.

The future looks bright. Watch for some really interesting connector designs this year!

================================

ABOUT THE AUTHOR

Robert Brenner is an engineer, consultant, college professor, and teacher with extensive experience in research and information publishing.

A retired Navy mustang (enlisted then officer) with 11 submarine deployments under his belt, he holds a BSEE from the University of New Mexico, an MSEE from the Naval Postgraduate School, and an MSEE from the University of Southern California.

He is a Very High Speed Integrated Circuit (VHSIC) microelectronics pioneer with service in defense R&D before dedicating his energies to writing books full time.

He has been a guest speaker at national conferences and symposiums and is the author of over 60 books including *Going Solar: A Homeowner's Experience*; *Solar Case Study: 5.0 kW Home Power Generator*; *Solar Case Study: 6.4 kW Home Power Generator*; *Solar Case Study: 7.4 kW Home Power Generator: How to Construct (and Use) the 45W Harbor Freight Solar Kit*, *Power Up! The Smart Guide to Home Solar Power* and two *How Solar Works* books: *Solar Cells and Solar Panels* and *Solar Powered Electric Generators*. He also wrote articles on business and computer applications including over 50 articles for *Survival Life.com* and *Survivorpedia*.com. He taught electronics at high school, and taught engineering at the college, university, and graduate school levels. A futurist, he enjoys the challenge of research and is currently sharing his knowledge through his writing and public presentations.

The author can be reached by email at rcbwrites@gmail.com.

================================

OTHER BOOKS BY THE AUTHOR

Backyard Solar: Off-Grid Electrical Applications
    Bartering Basics: How to Trade for Food, Products, and Services
    Bigfoot Encounters in Michigan's Thumb: Sightings & Evidence of Sasquatch Presence
    Describing Action
    Describing People
    Describing Things
    Descriptive Language for Writers, Editors, and Speakers
    How Solar Works: Solar Cells and Solar Panels
    How Solar Works: Solar Powered Electric Generators
    Michigan Bigfoot Encounters (Volume 1 Upper Peninsula)
    Power Up! The Smart Guide to Home Solar Power
    Pricing Tactics
    Solar Case Study: 5.0 kW Home Power Generator
    Solar Case Study: 6.4 kW Home Power Generator
    Solar Case Study: 7.4 kW Home Power Generator
    Solar Power: How to Construct (and Use) the 45W Harbor Freight Solar Kit
    Supernatural and Strange Happenings in the Family
    Survive a Power Outage: Emergency Lighting
    Writer's Guide to Descriptive Language